ATTRACTING AND DATING

THE *WRONG* MEN?

TIPS AND INSIGHTS

TO FREE YOURSELF

SIGNE A. DAYHOFF, PHD

Attracting and Dating the Wrong Men?
Tips and Insights to Free Yourself

By Signe A. Dayhoff, PhD

Copyright © 2015 by Signe A. Dayhoff, PhD
Published by Effectiveness-Plus Publications LLC
80 Paseo de San Antonio
Placitas, New Mexico 87043-8735

Cover design by randolene at fiverr.com, CanStockPhoto.com

All rights reserved

No part of this book may be reproduced, stored in a retrieval system, or transmitted in any form or by any means, electronic, mechanical photocopying, microfilming, recording, or otherwise, without written permission from the author, except for the inclusion of brief quotations in a review.

ISBN: 978-0-9910965-7-2

Disclaimer: This publication is designed to provide accurate information in regard to the subject matter covered. Names of people and some locations have been changed. Attempts have been made to verify the information provided. The author and the publisher assume no liability for errors, inaccuracies, or omissions. Any resulting slights are unintentional. Neither the author nor the publisher is rendering psychological or any other professional service. The instruction, ideas, and advice are not intended as a substitute for appropriate professional help. The author and publisher disclaim any responsibility or liability resulting from application of procedures presented or discussed in this book.

DEDICATION

This memoir is dedicated to all who have ever had an interaction or relationship with a "wrong" man. It is also to all those who are unknowingly approaching, entering, or in the middle of this problem. Few females have been taught how to assert themselves, be their own person, act on what *they* want in casual or romantic situations with men, and focus on what's in their own best interest. Even as this book is being published, years after my own personal experiences, the attracting and dating situation has changed very little for how women are expected to act—expected by men, themselves, and social custom. Attracting and dating presents a difficult world for men and women, one filled with invalid assumptions, misinformation, fear of negative evaluation and rejection, miscommunications, and lack of reality checks. So if any of this sounds or feels familiar, take heart. It happens to everyone. But the good news is that there are likely to be tips and insights in this book that will be useful to giving you a leg up on dealing with this knotty problem.

TABLE OF CONTENTS

PROLOGUE 1
1. CARNY 10
2. BRENT 18
3. MATTHEW 31
4. STEVE 43
5. ROBERT AND RICHARD 49
6. EDDIE 61
7. PHIL 72
8. BENNY 82
9. MARCELLO 109
10. TULLY 123
11. JESSIE 133
12. MARK 136
13. FRED 143
14. JOHN 147
15. TIM 151
16. TOM 154
17. RANDALL 158
18. BUFF COP 168
19. DOLAN 174
20. JIM 179
21. DR. HARVARD 189
22. HARVEY 192
23. DONALD 212
24. BILL 224
EPILOGUE 230
ABOUT THE AUTHOR 232

ACKNOWLEDGMENTS

No book becomes a reality without the encouragement of others. First I offer my thanks to my mother, Anne, who always had my back and kept motivating me to keep writing even when there seemed too many obstacles to overcome. Second, I offer my gratitude to the many who listened, cringing or chuckling (or both), to my tales of romantic disaster, quietly identifying with them. And third, I offer my continuing appreciation of Judith Sherven PhD and Jim Sniechowski PhD, well-known for their many *New York Times* best-sellers and their "Overcoming Fear of Being Fabulous" program, who read rough drafts, made insightful suggestions, and cheered me on.

PROLOGUE

I'm sure that most women who didn't marry while in high school or go directly into a religious order afterward have experienced attracting or dating at least one "wrong man" in their lives.

Perhaps he was wrong because you and he didn't have much in common or there was no chemistry. You thought, "No thanks," but he was a clinging pound puppy in need of rescuing. Because he was attracted to you, he dogged your footsteps, trying to get your attention and give him a puppy biscuit, unwilling to take "no" for an answer.

Or you and he seemed to have lots in common or there seemed to be knock-your-socks-off chemistry so you thought, "This could be fun!" But then you found yourself in a situation with a narcissist who wanted and needed to demonstrate his superiority and control over you, telling you what to do, always having to be right, judging you, and/or putting you down. Maybe Lesley Gore's "You Don't Own Me" came to mind.

Or you found yourself with a psycho who wanted ... who knows what he wanted... and put you in fear of your life or safety.

Or you found yourself with someone who fell in between, somewhere along the broad continuum of "wrong men"—someone who was unacceptably annoying, aggressive, untrustworthy, deceptive, dependent, or insecure, who acted with disrespect or unrealistic expectations. As a result, you wanted to escape but had difficulty comfortably doing so.

This is an autobiographical novel. Covering fifteen years of my life, it represents my experiences with attracting and dating the "wrong men." It demonstrates what I did, thought, felt, and discovered. It examines what underlay this problem for me, and for many women, and what awareness I needed before I could begin to address and resolve it. It provides tips and insights about how expectations of yourself as a female and loyalties to their "shoulds" that you learned in your childhood have influenced your interactions with males. Furthermore, it suggests how you can alleviate these negative expectations and loyalties to confidently interact with the "right" men. I experienced it as Erma Bombeck meets Dean Koontz.

I want to thank all these "wrong men" for motivating me to discover how shackled I was feeling having to meet *their* expectations. Their attitudes, beliefs, and behaviors dragged me kicking and screaming to examine what I had unconsciously been directed to believe that just didn't work for me. What I wanted in dating situations was to be respected and accepted as an individual, not expected to play some unconscious male-oriented, fawning female role.

As the stories that follow point out, attracting and dating the wrong men can put you in situations rife with crazy making, fear, irritation, sadness, frustration, disappointment, manipulation, and danger. If you're like most women, these situations have tended to leave you unsure how you can easily extricate yourself from them with confidence, finesse, and safety the next time you interact with a "wrong man." They may also have left you feeling guilty and responsible for your plight. However, because you found yourself in any of these situations does *not* mean that you were to blame for them.

The cold reality is that "attracting and dating the wrong men" situations are often difficult to avoid, much less handle well, because of conscious and unconscious expectations that have been taught to you about how you "should" think and act around men. That is, even if you are a strong, assertive, confident woman with good social decision-making skills, and a Black Belt in karate, you can still struggle with expectations about how you "should" think and act. That is, even if you were a Wonder Woman—with your star-emblazoned, patriotic hot pants and Golden Girdle of Gaea for strength, you would still tend to have this nagging, underlying expectation problem.

According to your culture, parents, teachers, television, advertising, or your church, females "should" be attractive, demure, agreeable, compassionate, submissive, accommodating, *and* frame everything they do in attraction-and-dating interactions around the *man's* expectations of them. These are gender-role expectations which were implanted in your brain in early childhood, continuously reinforced, and later emphasized in your adolescence as you approached dating-related female-male interactions.

When you have any of these female gender-role beliefs embedded in the back of your skull, as I did, you will have an unconscious allegiance to them. With these allegiances, or loyalties, have come forbiddances. These are what you cannot allow yourself to do as a result of these unconscious expectations about what you "should" do. They hold you back. Under their spell, you tend to react to situations with men with a degree of dependence, uncertainty, conflict, stress, and unassertiveness which often embroils you in difficult circumstances.

Consequently, you will tend to feel in a quandary about the "right" way to handle these circumstances. You will believe you "should" do certain things in a certain prescribed way in interactions with men irrespective of how you may personally feel. You will tend to believe you have to be nurturing, always caring and understanding with men which can leave you tending to be unable to quickly, kindly, and effectively dispose of these man-related problems. This can leave you with a sense of inadequacy in this realm and unnecessary guilt about your less-than-successful handling of these problems.

Signe A. Dayhoff, PhD

It took me fifteen years to learn that I did not know how to handle situations with men satisfactorily. Like most women, I had never been taught in school or in my home how to be my own independent person: how to recognize these obstructive beliefs and discard them; how to be socially effective in my interpersonal relationships; how to assertively deal with conflict; how to make confident, informed decisions for myself; and how to solve and deal with these tricky male-female relationship problems before they got out of hand.

These attracting-dating stories detail what happened to me, what I thought at the time, what I did as a result, and how I became aware of my unconscious expectations, allegiances, and forbiddances. Some of my interactions with men were crazy, some humorous, some sweet but conflict-ridden, some frustrating, some angry, and some just plain scary. The stories also show how my increasing rejection of those negative expectations, allegiances, and forbiddances changed my thinking and behavior in those situations from inadequate to productive. They highlight my journey through a transformation, revealing my battle to become aware of my own lack of knowledge and skills as well as the strictures of unconscious beliefs that had shackled me.

Years after my experiencing the last of these adventures, I had high hopes that women of a younger age would be starting from where I had left off—no longer riddled with unconscious gender-role beliefs and fears of being negatively evaluated for being themselves. I wanted to believe that the culture had truly changed, that women had come a long way toward seeing themselves more as individuals, and less as the culturally-programmed expectations of men. I further hoped younger women would be showing signs of no longer strictly following the female dating gender-role of passivity, dependence, and submissiveness, doing what the men expected of them in order to be accepted by men. I wanted to believe that younger women had become able to give themselves permission to determine and act on what *they* wanted.

However, my hopes were dashed when I happened to see a couple of episodes of the *Millionaire Matchmaker* program on television. Suddenly it felt as if what I had hoped about women's gender-role progress was mostly illusory. Women now appeared to have been hypnotically time-regressed to the Dark Ages of my youth where the conscious and unconscious imperative was "do *whatever* is necessary to attract a man" and the women were buying it ... lock, stock, and breast implant.

Millionaire Matchmaker is a full-fledged female gender-role stereotyping reality show. Women are expected to wear short, tight, revealing dresses in order to "attract" the millionaire male clients of the matchmaker. The woman can be super-intelligent, have a fantastic personality, be a groundbreaking astrophysicist, and have more business and financial savvy than a Warren Buffett, but it's her cleavage and her very short, derriére-hugging dress that do the talking to sell her initially as a potential date.

On the show individuality is not something that is really prized. The matchmaker does look at some matching generalities but all the women appear to be essentially interchangeable except for color of hair or skin, height, weight, age, and ethnicity. This strikes me as a sad commentary in the 21st Century and what younger women tend to have to look forward to. Forget "You've come a long way, baby (and don't call me 'baby')."

There was one episode that epitomized how the real woman is not only ignored but also derogated and submerged in order to create some stereotyped "ideal female" impression that the male will find acceptable. I felt bad for a female millionaire-entrepreneur who was to be casually "matched" with one male millionaire.

This 38-year-old, thrice-married woman with children—we'll call her "Harriet"—was looking for someone who would be a fun, supportive companion, and, perhaps, her fourth husband. Owning a $3–5-million-dollar a year dance studio in California which taught pole dancing, she described herself as a "wild child," and looked it in her colorful, slightly avant-garde attire. But that's who she was. The matchmaker could choose to accept her or not as a female to be matched with her male clients. Harriet, who was very upfront about who she was and what she wanted, said she liked doing what she wanted to do. She was looking for someone who would appreciate her for expressing her true self.

The matchmaker, however, stated they would have to give Harriet a _total make-over_: hair, makeup, and clothing. She had to look a "certain" way ... period. They wanted to cut her hair. They argued. Harriet adamantly said "no." Instead, they straightened her hair—nearly all the women have longish, straight hair. They redid her make-up. Then they presented her with short, dark-colored, somewhat more conservatively-styled clothes to wear. Harriet said, "I think those look dowdy." She found them simply "not her style at all." She felt her potential date should know what he was getting into from the start, which seemed like a smart move to me.

In fact, her new, more stereotyped look was false advertising. Because it wasn't who she was, she would want to shed this carefully-designed snake skin as soon as she could if she and her "match" were to get to know each other and continue dating. So what the man saw initially was not what he would get over time. It was a case of "bait and switch," unnecessarily creating an unfair, confusing, anger-producing, and unacceptable situation for them both.

Through a one-way mirror, she had to pick a man who was good-looking to her and seemed potentially interesting. Unfortunately she would know very little about him. He, likewise, would view her in her new transformation and know very little about her except she had her own business. For all he would know she could be selling delicate, antique porcelain religious figurines or running a gambling casino-brothel. Theirs would truly be a "blind" date, one likely doomed to failure. Rather than the two individuals deciding together as equals what they would like to do on this first date, the matchmaker told the man, in his stereotyped role as leader and decision maker, to arrange it, which he did.

However, Harriet, on her own, decided she wanted to have some say. She asked him to meet her at her studio first before going to dinner. There she surprised him by personally performing a pole-dance. That was who she was. Moreover, that's what she did for a living: She taught other women to pole dance for fun and profit. It was a tasteful acrobatic demonstration and she was appropriately covered during her performance.

Her date, however, did not appear to be even remotely a "wild child." During her performance, he looked not only mortified and humiliated but also down-right squeamish. It was hard to tell if he were more in need of Pepto-Bismol or a barf bag. He looked to be poised to run screaming from her studio and, perhaps, wash this graphic memory out of his mind with a couple of stiff double Scotches.

It was obvious he had zero appreciation for how she made her living, what she found to be fun, or what she wanted to share with him. During dinner he expressed to her the breadth of his incredulity and disgust. Equating pole dancing with "stripping," he acted as if she had wriggled out of her costume and given him a sweaty lap dance in middle of Times Square at lunchtime. He obviously found her and what she did to be beyond the pale for someone he would even consider dating.

She told him that she thought he might get a kick out of it. I could see that some men would. Furthermore, she wanted to let him know who she "really" was, which she didn't think he would discover over a formal meal of chitchat. After he expressed his utter repulsion for her, the date ended in a resounding thud with her leaving. It was an unmitigated disaster for both of them. The expectations of neither one had been met. It was an embarrassing waste of time as well.

When Harriet met with the millionaire matchmaker for an evaluation of the date, the matchmaker roundly criticized her for what she had done. Harriet replied that she "likes being herself and wanted her date to know that and her." However, as a result of the browbeating Harriet received during this interview, she began to give in to the matchmaker's continuing criticism and pejorative "psychiatric assessment" that she "really wasn't looking for a husband." The matchmakers suggested Harriet's behavior was an exhibitionist's ego trip—about and for Harriet alone.

Finally Harriet caved in. She then "confirmed" what the show's host had seemingly wanted and expected to hear all along, "I guess I want to be married to myself." (In all honesty, isn't that what nearly everyone truly wants: To find someone who represents all the things you like about yourself and identify with?)

The matchmaker responded with a sneer, "Good," indicating rudely that she did not want to have anything more to do with this woman. Then she summarily dismissed Harriet from her office and her service.

* * *

The show has an expectation-reinforcing message for women of any age, but especially for young women. It says if you want to snag a date with *any* man, but especially a "millionaire"—what the show purports is every girl's Cinderella dream, you "should" not, under any circumstances, dare to be yourself. You "should" do what men want and *expect* you to do. You *"should"* meet *their* gender-role expectations of you. You do *not* have their permission to do anything else unless you want to be negatively evaluated and rejected.

Attracting and Dating the Wrong Men?

Later I discovered that the changes I had hoped had come about since I had "slipped the surly bonds of dating" were mostly imaginary—simply wishful thinking on my part. According to research, the female role expectations that had plagued my youth, and beyond, are still alive and well-entrenched. Revealing themselves in our interpersonal scripts, they have remained sadly consistent over the past decades.

This book is not a condemnation of men per se. The men in these stories acted as they did for their own personal, conscious and unconscious reasons, from their own histories, experiences, needs, wants, beliefs, allegiances, loyalties, forbiddances, emotions, cultural teachings, expectations, values, and/or problems. Furthermore, they acted in concert with my inability to assert myself, my ignorance of my loyalties, allegiances, forbiddances, and rights, the lack of skills necessary to exercise those rights, and act in my own best interests.

This book is, however, a condemnation of unfair cultural expectations for how women (and men) "should" act. It's a condemnation of the negative programming we all have received in our childhood, as roles rather than as individuals. Being unrealistic, these cultural expectations have made women-men attraction and dating so much harder, more conflict-ridden and stressful, and less satisfactory than they need to be.

* * *

Massachusetts

1

CARNY

It was a bright, sunny Saturday, the beginning of the summer following my freshman year at the Clyde F. Brown High School on Main Street in rural Millis. Not far from the school's two-story brick building a carnival had suddenly appeared on the school's grounds, fully constructed, almost as in a puff of smoke. After being transported by a caravan of trucks, large and small, it had been set up in the area that was relegated to the Millis Mohawks football games during the school year. Hauled in on flat-bed trucks were the six large rides, including a Ferris wheel. Roustabouts carefully unfolded them, bolted them together, and then rolled them into their pre-determined stationary locations within the carnival confines. The food and vendor stands, which had been pulled in on tow-behind trailers, mushroomed along the far side of the rides near the school's property line, perpendicular to the street.

Their independent food concessionaires furnished the cotton candy, caramel apples, hamburgers, hot dogs, snow cones, and a variety of soft drinks the carnival offered. Popcorn, however, had its own special two-wheeled, red popcorn circus wagon which was heavily decorated with gold filigree relief. The moment it started popping fresh popcorn kernels the air was filled with its tempting, fun-time-beckoning aroma. The traveling amusement show also included games of chance and skill where mostly males would try to demonstrate their spatial and athletic abilities and good luck. As soon as the carnival crew had it primed for customers, it radiated all the entrancing glitzy, gaudy sights and sounds you'd expect from a carnival show even during the daylight hours.

It was warm and humid when I entered the carnival grounds at noon to wander around the rides and booths. Everything was flashing lights and motion, with calliope music, the voices of hawkers, food smells, and the ever-present squeals of those experiencing fast or gravity-defying thrills. Dressed casually in belted, tan Bermuda shorts, three-quarter-length-sleeved white blouse, sneakers, and with my long, medium-blonde hair hanging down my back, I was checking everything out as a lark. I didn't have the money for the rides or games but I wanted to see all that they had to entice and enthrall.

At a booth near the entrance was an athletically-trim, muscular young man with sandy-hair and blue eyes, wearing jeans and a tight-fitting white tee-shirt which revealed part of a tattoo on his right upper arm. Probably around thirty, he was standing in front of the counter at a ring-toss game booth. He reminded me of David Nelson in *The Adventures of Ozzie & Harriet*. There he was demonstrating to everyone walking by how "easy" it was to pitch the sisal rings so they landed encircling the individual milk bottles situated in rows on a table behind him, gaining them a prize. Over and over again with a subtle flick of the wrist he sailed the rings the four-to-five-foot distance onto their targets, slipping them just over the lips of the bottles to keep them from being hung up in between. As I paused to inspect his game, he spoke to me. Surprisingly, it was not to invite me to play. Instead, he struck up a conversation.

"It's such a beautiful day. If I weren't here, I would probably spend it fishing by a quiet stream or maybe sitting in a rowboat floating along. I really like the water. How about you? If you weren't here, what would you be doing?"

I laughed, "I don't know. Maybe reading or writing. I do that a lot."

"What do you like to read?"

"Mostly novels—you know, Hemingway and Faulkner—and some non-fiction.

"Who do you like better?"

"I guess I like Hemingway for the action stories but Faulkner for the rich description."

"So what do you think of our little carnival so far?"

"I'm impressed. I can't imagine traveling from place to place with all this equipment, putting it up and taking it down again. How long does it take to set up once you arrive?"

"Several hours generally. Everybody pitches in though only certain people are allowed to check out the rides to make sure they are safe. We try to get to each location at night so we can set up the rides very early in the morning and then get all the booths ready. How about you? Do you go to the high school here?" His hand swept left toward the brick building just off the street. Then he went back to his tossing the rings.

"I just finished my freshman year. We're going to be moving into a new school building soon. It's under construction now and supposed to be ready for fall." I pointed to my right beyond the line of trees. "If you don't mind my asking, how did you happen to come to work with this carnival? Are you doing it just at this location or do you always work with them?"

Just then two couples approached where the males were acting as if they were going to show their female companions how it was really done. What surprised me was that as they came forward and watched for a few moments, they apparently didn't take the time to notice exactly how the game operator was tossing the rings. I had to smile to myself as the young men tossed the rings with too much strength, loft, and distance in trying to show off for their companions. The harder they tried, the worse they did. There was no calculated, subtle flick of the wrist in evidence. So after several rounds each, the guys gave up. Grumbling that the game was probably fixed, they acceded to the prompting of their female companions to find something more "successful" for winning them a stuffed animal, and moved on.

"You were going to tell me about how you came to work with the carnival," I said.

"Oh, it was nothing I'd planned to do. I went straight into the Navy out of high school. It was the thing to do at the time." He continued tossing the rings. "I was in three years when the Korean War started. I was assigned to the cruiser *USS Rochester* which was involved in the amphibious invasion of Inchon, North Korea. That resulted in recapturing Seoul and was a strategic reversal for the U.N."

"So, you were really in the thick of things. Sounds exciting and scary."

"Yeah, it was. Then after a total of eight years in the Navy, I got out, landing in Virginia. I was looking around, trying to figure out what to do with myself, where I'd fit in with the skills I had. This carnival was passing through the area, working its way north. Like most of them, it winters in Florida. I checked them out. They needed a hand so I took the job. I've been with them ever since. It's not a bad place to work, really. Sometimes it's hard constantly being on the move but you get used to it. At this point, I don't know what else I would do anyway. And, how about you? What about your plans for after high school?"

"Since I was little, I've wanted to be a doctor so that's what I'm aiming for. But it takes lots of years to do it."

"That's impressive. But, yeah, it does sound like lots of long, hard work. Say, would you like to sit down and get out of the sun while we chat?" He paused in his wrist action to point to a metal folding chair inside his booth in the shade. "You might be a little cooler and more comfortable. I'll keep tossing the rings if you don't mind."

"Sure. Thanks. That's very thoughtful of you." I took him up on his offer as he snagged the individual bottles perfectly every time.

At that moment a heavy-set man with longish, wavy, gray-streaked black hair and an aquiline nose was making his way toward us. He stopped and leaned against the side of the booth. "Hey, Mike," he said, "you oughta have the little lady shill for ya." He pointed his thumb in my direction then turned to face me, "How's about it, sweetheart? You wanna do Mike a big favor and give a big smile to all the men who walk by? Bring the crowds in for him? Make 'em want to show you how good they are?"

Mike stopped tossing. Suddenly he moved toward the fat man. His face was red with anger. Pressing his tense, hard upper torso into the older man's softer gut, he said through clenched teeth, "Look, Gino! This is a nice girl. Keep your nasty comments to yourself around her."

The heavy-set man snickered and shook his head, unimpressed. Mike stepped back as if chastised and reluctantly began tossing again. As the intruder turned on heel to walk away, he said to Mike with a theatrical wink and mocking laugh, "So you think you're gonna get lucky with her, do ya?"

As the man left, Mike turned to me looking abashed, "That's the carnival boss. Ignore him. He's a big jerk." Pausing to regain his composure, he asked, "How about some lemonade? You must be thirsty."

"No, thanks a lot. Maybe I should move along. I don't want you to get in trouble because of your talking to me."

"Yeah, well, maybe so," he said, looking in Gino's direction. "But you could always stop by later if you're here and say, 'Hi.' Which reminds me, did you know there's a contest tonight? Yeah, they're going to be picking a 'Miss Millis' from the local girls. You really ought to enter. They even have a crown."

Embarrassed, I said, "No, I don't think so. That's not me."

"Sure it is."

But as I thought about it for another moment, it occurred to me that there might be some money involved. On the off-chance I might win, maybe I should consider it. "Does it cost to enter? What would I have to do in this contest?"

"No, it's free. Wear something nice, smile, and be yourself. You'd be the winner hands down." I smiled self-consciously at his enthusiasm.

When I left, I began rolling the contest over in my mind. A small cash prize could help my family's situation a little. Because of my father's emotional problems and resulting spotty employment record we were constantly skirting financial disaster.

That evening I convinced my mother to drive me back to the carnival. I reappeared there with my hair in soft curls down my back, wearing a sleeveless dress of navy blue, lavender, and white in a muted abstract design on polished cotton with a fitted bodice, full skirt over a sewn-in petticoat, with white high heels.

Mike saw me immediately as I entered and gave me an approving nod. "You look great. You'll knock 'em dead!"

When the "contest" was called, there were only five of us who had entered. What we had to do was one by one walk into a fifteen-foot diameter grassy circle, walk its circumference, and then walk back out. It surprised me that I was the only one who was all dressed up for it. So I threw back my shoulders, sucked in my gut which stuck out my 34-A chest, and did my best runway-model promenade. I smiled and pirouetted once, twirling my full skirt, as I walked around the circle. I was also the only one who seemed to take full advantage of this self-presentation opportunity.

Who the judges were I didn't know for sure. I thought they might have been some of the town government people (men) responsible for bringing the carnival here. The decision of the judges didn't take much time. To the applause and cheers of those who had crowded around, *I* was crowned "Miss Millis."

Following that announcement, the carnival boss took me aside. I wasn't sure what he was going to say given our earlier encounter. Confidentially he explained, "The Miss Millis crown has been broken so you won't get it." I had no idea if there really had been a crown to begin with, based upon what my father had said about "the evils of carnival people, their lies and manipulations." But I didn't care about a crown. Instead, he informed me, "In its place you are receiving two free passes for the Ferris wheel and ten dollars in cash." Okay. It wasn't as much as I'd have hoped for but it was a far sight better than a crown.

Just then one of the judges tapped the carnival boss on the shoulder, "Come on, Gino, don't be such a piker. At least give her another ten." He did, but grudgingly. I gave the tickets to my mother and younger brother so they could ride together and held the twenty for her for later. As they rose into the air to begin their sky-hugging revolutions, I wandered back to Mike's booth which was crowded with ring-toss "experts."

With a grin on his face, he said, while passing out the sisal rings, "See, I knew you could do it. Congratulations, 'Miss Millis'"

I turned as many shades of red as my embarrassment would allow. "Thanks. And I want you to know it's been fun talking with you." I hung back watching people toss the rings.

"Thanks. Yeah, me too."

When my mother and brother were ready to leave, I nodded good-bye. Mike stood at attention and gave me a snappy naval salute while watching the last of his customers exercise their skills. Shortly after we had headed home at ten o'clock, the carnival began packing up to leave that night for Marlborough to set up again the next day. Then they were off to Chelmsford, Tewksbury, Methuen, on to New Hampshire and then to Maine. Mike's sweet behavior toward me, however, remained behind.

* *

Resulting Awareness: My father's generalizations about carnival folk made me see a discrepancy between what he expected and what I experienced. Specifically, he was attributing particular attitudes and behaviors to every member of that group. But Mike as an individual had been friendly and gentlemanly—not representative of that stereotype. This started me further questioning the validity of my father's other beliefs, expectations, and stereotypes. Thinking about Mike, I realized that he had been too old and too worldly for me if I had had any thoughts about dating him, which I hadn't. But what I found interesting was that in talking with him as simply another person who happened to be male instead of as a potential date, I felt less compelled to adhere to the dictates of how I was supposed to act as a female.

The question I asked myself: What did this awareness have for the many other things I had been taught and led by my father to believe, that didn't match my experiences?

* * *

2

BRENT

When I was a junior at Millis High School, I worked after class and on weekends at Sunshine Dairy where I encountered lots of "wrong" men. One day a tall, lean, sandy-haired, young man named Brent—who could have been a poster-child for "Young America"—stopped by the luncheonette. A freshman at Northeastern University, he was on his way back home from a Saturday baseball game in nearby Milford. Sweaty and dusty, he was heading to Natick but not before he had a bite to eat and something to quench his thirst. As he walked in, he immediately caught my attention. I was impressed by his stature, physique, and poise. The way he stood at the door glancing around, as if surveying his kingdom, suggested to me he expected I would be impressed.

    Sunshine Dairy had been called Furlong's when I first moved to Millis a little over three years before. Selling sodas and ice cream, it was the local hangout for all the teens after school, but especially on a Saturday night where the parking lot was filled with cars, cigarette smoke, soft drinks, beer, and raucous laughter. Sold to the Geoghegans who already had their first ice cream store in Framingham, it was then painted white and refurbished inside with updated booths. It no longer reminded me of a grooving Beatnik watering hole, where bad lighting eliminated the need for any kind of décor.

Attracting and Dating the Wrong Men?

Seating himself at the counter, he examined the menu and appeared ready for something other than just ordering. After we exchanged only a few words of introduction, he asked me out over his hamburger and French-fried onion rings. It was the first time I had ever experienced anything that quick or that confident. On the rare occasions when I was asked for a date, it was usually by young men who had already been graduated from high school, who had gone into business or had become collegians with professions in mind. The young men in my classes asked me out infrequently. It was, perhaps, because I appeared a little aloof, the result of my overly-critical father often reminding me of how flawed I was.

Awkwardly, I couldn't give Brent a definitive answer at that moment. Generally speaking, my parents met my date when he came to pick me up. But while my father generally would have found Brent's clean-cut 1950's image instantly praiseworthy, I didn't want anyone to meet my father in his current state of cycling between mania and depression. Instead, I requested my mother check him out at other than our second-floor apartment on east Main Street. Somewhat tentatively, I inquired, "Would you mind if I brought my mother to meet you?"

He chuckled with a strained, patronizing look, "No, of course not. That would be fine. I understand the problem." *You* understand the problem? I wondered how he could possibly. Then he added, "I work weekends and some evenings at the main Sunshine Dairy in Framingham. You and your mother could meet me there."

"When will you be working there next?"

"This Sunday afternoon, noon to five. Is that time enough for you?"

"Sure. We'll see you then."

I re-arranged my hours for Sunday so I could be out of my fried-clam-slinging uniform and grease-smeared industrial apron for a couple of hours to take Mother to meet him. I was working at Sunshine Dairy because the job had become available when the Furlong's renovation occurred and I desperately needed the money. But I hated the permanent stench of grease that clung to everything, including my skin, hair, and the interior of "my" birthday-present-used-car I shared with my mother for work. Fortunately I didn't have to convince my mother to meet him. She thought it would be great fun.

After scrubbing off the rank odor of hamburgers, fried clams, French fries, and deep-fried onion rings, I dressed casually. I wanted to create a positive but uncompetitive impression of myself as I trailed after my very attractive and stylish mother. She was five-seven, slim, with short strawberry-blonde hair, sparkling blue eyes, and a peachy complexion, wearing a brownish red lipstick that set off her coloring dramatically. She always dressed simply but elegantly on very little money. In fact, she could make any outfit, even rolled-up jeans, a man's shirt with shirttail tied at the waist, and sneakers, look fashionable. There was no question she would turn heads at the dairy, including Brent's. He had no idea what to expect. That thought tickled me.

In the Framingham store we made our way through the crowd to the only remaining seats, two red-plastic-covered bar stools at the pale aqua Formica lunch counter. Brent was busy juggling orders of fried clams, ice cream sundaes, and hamburgers. When he saw me, he smiled. But when he saw my mother, he did a double-take. My heart skipped a couple of beats. As soon as he had served his current customers, he sauntered over and said "Hello" to me but locked eyes with my mother, obviously appraising her.

"Mrs. Dayhoff—or would it be too presumptuous of me to ask if I might call you 'Anne'—I am so glad to meet you. I'm pleased you could come by today. Signe has told me so much about you. You certainly exceed all my expectations."

Mother smiled, even blushed a little, as she accepted his compliment. But her smile belied an awareness of his tactics. "Call me 'Mrs. Dayhoff,'" she replied pleasantly.

Undeterred, he continued, "By the way, did you catch the fragrance of the blossoms on the rose bushes near the door as you entered? I understand you used to grow old garden roses. I wish I could grow them where I live." He was babbling, using my answers to questions he had asked about her ahead of time: What did she like? What did she do?

He paused to let it sink in then, then seemingly as an after-thought said, "But let me take your orders first and then you can tell me your secret." I beseeched Heaven to spare me but Brent didn't notice. He was totally focusing on Mother instead of on me. We ordered tuna salad sandwiches on toasted rye and iced tea with lemon. Aside from my saying what I wanted to eat, I was rendered virtually indiscernible from the tables and chairs behind me since I was not his audience. But even though I knew he was ingratiating himself with her to make a good impression, I felt awkward sitting there as he drank in my mother, as if preferring her to me. It occurred to me he actually might be. She was a stunner and was playing her role as a "serious seeker of wisdom and truth" to the hilt.

He was all charm and sincerity. "I also understand that you knit professionally, that you've made sweaters of all kinds." Mother hardly had a chance to touch her lunch for all the courtly attention he paid her when he wasn't attending to other customers. She was enjoying her role of the Queen Mother with this young knight groveling at her feet.

As Brent poured it on, it was as if he took it for granted she couldn't possibly say "no" to all this gallantry and my going out with this Sir Galahad. The degree of his interpersonal savvy amazed me. There was no question in my mind this guy was going places. But in architecture which he was studying? No. He should have been going into politics.

Mother gave me a subtle smile. His being all over her like a cloying perfume was certainly not lost on her. She knew precisely what he was doing and to a degree appreciated that his efforts, albeit heavy-handed, were in the right direction. Besides, it was a kick being on the receiving end of his overblown chivalric maneuvers—not something she would experience again any time soon. He was young, still perfecting his technique, but it was, after all, a "technique."

Just as we finished, we exchanged winks. I signaled Brent. Speaking for only a moment at the cash register, we made tentative plans for next Saturday afternoon. Maybe I should use my mother as my calling card even when it was no longer necessary ...but, then again, maybe not.

During the week Brent called to say that our first date was confirmed to be at an all-day party at his friend Charley's house in Natick. I was excited. He seemed too good to be true: Suave, or at least as suave as a college freshman could be, courteous, intelligent, and good looking. It took me awhile to decide what I should wear. It was casual. It probably wasn't a slacks, pedal pushers, or Capri pants activity, so I picked out navy culottes. With them I wore a short-sleeved blue button-down Oxford-cloth shirt, stockings, and my cordovan Bass Weejun loafers.

My waist-length hair was clean and shiny. After a sleepless night of large, pink plastic curlers painfully indenting themselves in my scalp, I had spent about twenty minutes carefully styling my hair so it flowed in soft, seductive waves from the crown of my head down my back, tickling my waist. It was just right. I knew I would pass inspection with Brent and his friends with flying colors.

Brent picked me up at twelve-thirty in his silver Pontiac. Initiating the conversation, I shared, "My mother was impressed with you." I expected him to say, "Thank you" or "I'm glad," or "Good" so I wasn't prepared for his response.

Attracting and Dating the Wrong Men?

"I thought she would be," he smiled knowingly. "It's all in what you do and how you do it. I sweet-talked her and swept her right off her feet. And it worked, didn't it? She had no choice but to let you go out with me. How could she have said 'no'?"

You talked her into it? I thought, astounded. What a chuckle! Apparently he hadn't considered the possibility that as long as he wasn't rude or unwashed, and didn't drool, snort, fart, or pick lint out of his navel, she was going to go along with *my* prior judgment of him irrespective, that the meeting was only a matter of form.

Thirty minutes later we were on a heavily-treed street with small, mostly-white two-story houses having been built in the late 1940s or early 1950s. Each had its own cramped but neat patch of mowed front lawn surrounding a large maple tree. Charley's yard was interspersed with groupings of colorful flowers—begonias, impatiens, pansies, petunias, red and blue salvia—along the front walkway and lilacs and forsythia along the foundation of the house. After Brent parked, we strolled down the sidewalk and the fifteen-foot concrete path to the screen door. A breeze lovingly played with my hair. I felt all was right with the world. I was feeling good, looking my best, and with an attractive guy as my date. Things couldn't have been better. But as we approached Charley's door, I let out a scream.

A terrorist pigeon had flown over me and—splat—had released its organic payload squarely on the top of my head!

I was so shocked I wasn't even embarrassed. "Oh, my God! Get me to the nearest bathroom!" I urged Brent, wanting to cover the top of my head with my hand but not wanting to touch it.

"What?" He hadn't seen the bombardier drop what seemed emotionally to me like the equivalent of "Little Boy" over Hiroshima. Now I had to explain what had happened. The vision suddenly burst upon him. "Oh," he responded, curling his upper lip in disgust. All I wanted to do was scrub my scalp ... now. Later I could work to recover from my humiliation and try to salvage the date.

Once inside the house, Brent found Charley's mother. Recoiling at my predicament, she escorted me into the cramped downstairs half-bath under the stairs to the second floor, with its inadequate light over the sink. There she supplied me with a wash cloth and some shampoo. As I looked in the mirror at myself, I could imagine all sorts of parasites crawling all over my head. I shuddered in repugnance. The bird's droppings were still warm as I tried to locate the spinach-and-mayonnaise-looking mess which I couldn't see clearly without the use of a second mirror.

After using toilet paper to wipe it up, I tried to rinse the area under the low-set faucet then scrubbed and scrubbed and scrubbed with shampoo. Even though it was likely that no more than a teaspoon of excrement had landed on me, I had no idea if I were getting it all or, perhaps, if I were merely spreading it around. So I worked in an ever-widening circle. After awhile, I forced myself to stop my compulsivity. What I really needed was a shower. Attempting to repeatedly, awkwardly rinse the top of my head, I had managed to erase all recognition of my previous coiffure. What was worse, I still had no idea to what degree I had actually expunged the bird's droppings or rinsed out the suds. With the hand towel, I dried, as best I could, all my sopping hair on top, sides, and partially down in back, leaving it flat, damp, and peculiarly stringy looking. Those long, flowing, romantic tresses that I had so painfully created had been totally eliminated. Grimacing as I stared into the mirror, I needed more than some conditioner, a proper hair dryer, and curling iron. I needed a large hat.

I had been secreted in this cubbyhole for at least ten minutes. Combing my hair back from my face and wishing I had had hair pins to put it up on top of my head, I finally dragged myself out into the gathering. Looking more than a little the worse for wear, I searched for Brent. He was socializing with everyone. I sidled up to him in the living room.

"You get it all taken care of?" he asked. Thankfully he didn't mention in front of those assembled what I had to take care of or emphasize the dramatic before-and-after difference in my appearance. However, those circled around him looked at me strangely, some with slight smiles or furrowed brows. I wondered if it was because I looked so soggy and bedraggled or he had told them, in his own inimitable way, about his date having been ingloriously "shat" upon.

"I certainly hope so," I replied, smiling, trying to look insouciant, as if nothing out of the ordinary had happened: "Pigeons? I laugh at pigeons. Ha, ha! Take that!" with a snap of my fingers.

He led me to the soft drinks and chips, dips, and sandwich makings on the beige Formica counter near the stove in the kitchen. Then he wandered off again. The oblong maple kitchen table had been pulled over next to the opposite wall. Several people were gathered around it, talking, picking out albums that were stacked on top of it. They glanced at me for longer than a second then resumed their activity. The table held a phonograph which was blasting the Rusty Warren's album, *Knockers Up*. Beside it were other, more sexually-explicit albums available for playing by some male, whose name I didn't recognize.

Despite my not having had lunch and feeling hungry, I grabbed only a can of Seven-Up and a mouthful of Fritos and moved along quickly. The music wasn't my taste. The sound was deafening. Moreover, I didn't want to stand there eating by myself, or, worse, awkwardly carry a sandwich with me. I wandered around the heavily-populated, moving mass of late-teens talking and laughing until I finally spied Brent. This time he was in the den amusing those surrounding him with his witty baseball stories. Now I was thinking that instead of taking up politics, he should consider becoming a raconteur like Jean Shepherd. When he was "on," he was both captivating others and thoroughly enjoying himself.

For a first date we spent only fleeting moments together despite the hours we were at Charley's. He was more engrossed with his listeners than with me. As the afternoon wore on, I wasn't sure why he had asked me to come along. Was I there simply so he wouldn't be seen without a "date"? Or was he now distancing himself from me because of the pigeon's kiss of death?

When he finally took me home, things didn't improve. Standing inside the main front door for the two apartments, he tried to kiss me. But I inadvertently turned my head at that precise moment, resulting in his smacking his lips hard into my nose instead, dislodging my glasses which almost fell onto the floor. He recovered quickly and followed up with a small, tentative smooch on my cheek. To my surprise none of what had transpired at Charley's or afterward seemed to have dissuaded him from suggesting a second date. When we set it up during the week by phone, I hoped I would get more of his attention the second time around.

On our second date we went to Nantasket Beach, northeast of Hingham, with a group of six others he knew, all of us crammed into his Pontiac. The water there was cold and invigorating, the air salty-fresh, the sand pristine, the sun warm, and the company full of fun. It was a day suited to time together. But Brent tended to be more interested in the beach volleyball competition than in me.

I'm not sure what I expected, but it hardly seemed like a date at all. It was more like a brother-sister outing except for his giving me a kiss as we sat on a colorful cotton blanket on the sand between games having lunch. While he was at his athletic best, I wasn't. In high school I played softball and basketball but had rarely played volleyball and so couldn't play it at all. I didn't even know I was supposed to have my hands together and bump the ball with my forearms to propel it over the net. No one volunteered to show me what to do. Finally, because I was losing our team points, I let someone else with more experience and more finely-tuned skills cover my slot as well as their own. Instead, I spent my time watching.

As the sun was sinking lower in the flamingo-pink sky, Brent and the other boys began their males-only moving game of catch down the beach. I began chatting with the other females, as we sat on our respective blankets, about what we were each currently doing. With one named Amy, who likewise had taken high school French, I tried to communicate in the language. It was an abysmal failure with us resorting to a flurry of gestures to try to fill in all our noun and verb gaps, giggling at our truly pathetic efforts. Even though Brent didn't seem pleased I hadn't remained fully immersed in being his cheering squad of one, he did ask for a third date as he dropped me off home.

My classmate Marilyn was giving a party at her home on the following Saturday evening. Everyone in my class was going, with or without dates. I invited Brent as my date. Because of his work schedule, he suggested we arrive separately, although I was willing to wait for him to pick me up. My best friend Margie and I had positioned ourselves near the door to greet guests as they arrived and talk. We wanted to compare notes about our upcoming senior year and future plans. I hadn't told her yet about Brent. He was my secret. I wanted to get her unbiased opinion of him later.

When he arrived, my wide, welcoming smile slid off my face. For some unfathomable reason Brent hadn't come alone. He had brought his friend, Jeff, also from Natick and who had been one of the six others at the beach the week before. I was more confused than angry at this unanticipated situation. Our coming in separate cars didn't change our being on a date, at least as far as I was concerned. I wanted to inquire but I let it go because it felt too embarrassing. Furthermore, I was afraid of seeming pushy. Whatever his reason, I felt he should have asked me beforehand if it would be all right.

The four of us talked awhile, laughing at Brent's stories, adding our own little anecdotes whenever we could squeeze them in. Then Brent asked me to dance. I thought, "Now we're getting somewhere." He was as smooth a dancer as he was a talker. We floated together to the Skyliners' "Since I Don't Have You." Then while someone changed the record, we stood on the dance floor, his arms still around me. I thought this meant we would have another whirl or two. This was like the date I had imagined. But, instead, he suggested I dance with Jeff. I was stunned. As the music resumed, he started walking me over to where Jeff and Margie were already engaged in an animated conversation.

"Margie," he said, as he extended his hand to hers, "I want you to dance with me."

Margie smiled brightly at Brent and they walked into the party room while I looked on, mouth agape. When Jeff asked me to dance, we followed. Brent was now showing Margie all his Gene Kelly-style dance moves. They were laughing and enjoying themselves. After shuffling unrhythmically around the room to Sam Cooke's "You Send Me," Jeff and I took a break to retrieve some potato chips and Cokes. Standing against a wall, he told me all about his studies at Pratt Institute, a design school in Brooklyn, New York, and how he was planning to become a commercial illustrator.

When he finally took a breath several songs later, I glanced around for a sign of Brent. He and Margie were no longer on the dance floor. I had no idea when they had left but assumed he must have cornered her somewhere, bestowing upon her his program of humorous stories. At this point I really wanted to reconvene the four of us in order to reconfigure the twosomes. Introducing Jeff to several of my classmates, I then excused myself for a few minutes to search for my missing date and best friend.

No one I asked, who wasn't engaged in making out, had seen Margie. She and Brent weren't on the back patio or in the backyard. They weren't in the front yard. I didn't see his Pontiac but I had no idea where he had parked. Seemingly Brent and Margie had disappeared. Now I wished I had told Margie ahead of time about Brent. However, even though she had been totally unaware of my having invited him as my date, he wasn't.

Time passed slowly. Jeff and I chatted with others. When Brent and Margie didn't reappear by the end of the party, I realized I had been ignominiously dumped. Moreover, Brent had apparently brought Jeff along to be my designated "date" in case he could change partners. This meant he likewise had assigned me to be Jeff's transportation home. That was truly adding insult to injury. But making it even worse, Jeff, in a display of incredible tackiness, tried for third base when I pulled up to his house. Was this Jeff's own idea or had Brent suggested it? At this point it didn't really matter. Brent's slick maneuvering had stunned me. If he had changed his mind about me, why didn't he just cancel the date? Or he could even have finished out this date as arranged then merely not asked me for another. I was no longer impressed by him.

Maybe my having survived pigeon bombardment with great aplomb wasn't such a ringing endorsement after all. It was no eye-opener that I never heard from Brent again. Years later, however, I discovered that he and Margie had clicked and become an "item" that night and had remained so for some years thereafter. But it wasn't until several decades later at one of our high school reunions that I asked her about him and told her what he had done. While she hadn't been aware of that particular incident, she had become privy to Brent's proclivities and, thus, had sent him on his way years before.

After my abandonment at Marilyn's, it occurred to me that maybe that pigeon's bomb drop was an omen, trying to tell me something. Too bad I couldn't have interpreted that nuclear splat more accurately and sooner.

* *

Resulting Awareness: For the first time I discovered that while attraction and dating is an exercise of mixing and matching, some individuals play it as a game. This makes it at the expense of others because only that player's skills and enjoyment count. I was naïve, totally unaware of this aspect of male-female relations. I had followed my role according to what was expected of me and found that it hadn't prepared me to recognize this degree of narcissism or expect this degree of manipulation. But even if I had, I had no idea how to deal with it so I could stay within my role expectations *and,* at the same time, feel good about myself. Those two things never seemed compatible to me.

The question I asked myself: What fears were compelling me to do what I "should" when doing so was acting contrary to what I wanted to do?

* * *

3

MATTHEW

One Sunday in August after my having been graduated from high school that June, I was still dishing out pistachio ice cream at Sunshine Dairy. Two young men entered, garbed in riding gear, appearing to be straight out of a photo spread from *Town and Country* magazine. The tall, blond one, who looked a little like a young Robert Redford in the *Twilight Zone* episode of "Nothing in the Dark," had on a white, high-collar show shirt, and jodhpurs, those tight-fitting trousers that reach to the ankle and end in the short jodhpur boots. The other one, who was shorter, likewise had on his show shirt and riding breeches but wore the long leather field boots and a low-profile equestrian helmet. All that was missing was their black competition riding coats, riding crops, and a British call of "Talley ho!" I hadn't heard about any competition in the area and wondered if people wore those outfits during practice or outside the ring. Since it was probably ninety degrees and seventy-percent humidity, they were definitely sweating profusely in their costumes.

The shorter one took off his helmet. He looked like a cross between a young Burt Reynolds and Dennis Weaver. His wet hair was dark and coarse, mostly standing straight up, lying flat, or adrift in a world of its own. They sat and introduced themselves as Charles and Matthew. Matthew, the dark-haired one, however, did all the talking from there on out, giving me what sounded like a sales pitch.

Even before ordering, he asked, "Would you like to learn how to ride a horse? It's so simple. I can teach you. We'd take it slow and easy. I guarantee you wouldn't fall off. You could even use a Western saddle instead of an English one if you felt you needed to hold onto the horn for safety. No galloping, no trotting, just a nice, leisurely walk at first. I could even lead you around until you became more comfortable. I'm a great, experienced teacher. I know you'd love it. What do you say? Want to give it a try?"

My first reaction was to look at him curiously. I wanted to ask, "Since when do they sell riding lessons door-to-door like encyclopedias?" But I held my tongue. Being appropriately demure, I simply said with only a hint of a smile, "No, thanks, I already know how."

"Okay. Well then, how would you like to come watch us ride? We will be participating in a show in a couple of months but you could watch us practice. We can show you all our fancy show moves. We're pretty impressive in the saddle and can get the horses to do just about anything but prepare and serve you dinner. You'd be amazed by what we can do." He chuckled to himself "What do you say to that?"

My mind was whirling. Is he kidding? "No, thanks."

He chuckled, "Well, in that case, how about *I* buy you dinner instead. We can leave the horses, riding, watching, and the competition for another time?"

That caught me off balance. It sounded to me like the foot-in-the-door sales technique: getting me to reject a big request so I'd be more likely to accept a smaller one. "I'll have to think about it," I answered, "How about I take your order," pointing at the menus. They both ordered fried clam sandwiches on hot dog buns and large Cokes.

Mulling over his odd invitation, I dumped raw clams into beaten eggs then into seasoned flour and then into the basket to be set into the bubbling oil in the deep-fat fryer. I wasn't sure what to say. He struck me as astoundingly egocentric to be much fun. But, then again, I hadn't been out in a quite while. Dinner would be a change, something to do. Moreover, I was leaving for Baylor University in Waco, Texas, with the goal of starting the long haul toward putting an "M.D." behind my name. Besides, staying home was not preferable to being out with this jerk. Listening to my father verbally abuse my mother, as he abused me, and not being able to do anything about it was not an acceptable alternative. So I finally said, "Yes."

Next Saturday evening we went to a steakhouse in North Framingham on Route 9, just past the new library extension. The restaurant ambiance was inviting with low-level lighting and comfortably-spaced, cloth-covered tables, each with its own small bouquet of real flowers and a lighted candle. But the food was barely edible, eliciting a big thumbs-down for my unsolicited review. My sirloin was tough, the baked potato under-cooked, and the green beans were mushy. Mushy vegetables reminded me of the over-cooked institutional food served to patients in too many hospitals and nursing homes. Over this unexciting repast I listened to him tell me his entire, sleep-inducing, life history. He was a senior at Boston College, going for an engineering degree. While I was able to occasionally slip something into the one-sided conversation, I felt more like an interviewer for a magazine profile than a date.

Before the end of the meal, during which I wished I drank alcohol so I could have felt a buzz instead of listening to one, I wondered if I should refuse a further date if he asked. Of course he'd ask. This was not immodesty. As per expectations, I had listened politely to all he spewed forth for over an hour with a slight smile of interest plastered to my face, nodding at all the appropriate times. Who wouldn't have found that captivating. However, from my perspective everything about him was annoying, disconcerting, and frustrating, like wearing itchy-scratchy, wool long-underwear.

The problem was that, as a polite female, I was *supposed* to give him the benefit of the doubt. This was our first date and it was possible, though I thought it highly unlikely, that he was a little nervous, like me, and so he was prattling. Consequently, if he asked, I should give him a second chance despite my strong gut feelings about his attitude and behavior. If my strictly-traditional, male-chauvinist father had been there beside me actually monitoring my decision making process (as he always was in my head), he would have insisted upon it.

Since there was nothing better to do with September approaching, I did give him a second, ... a third, ... and a fourth chance as well. But things did not improve. He was increasingly vexing. Everything was about him: what he thought, what he liked, what he didn't, what he needed, what he wanted. Continuing this relationship until I flew south wasn't worth the stress. But that meant I'd have to tell him so directly. That was what I dreaded and truly struggled with.

One evening as we were walking down the aisle in the Loews movie theater in Natick, he made an unpardonable error. We had come to see the Cinerama *How the West Was Won*, one of the last of the old-fashioned epic Westerns. Before the bright overhead lights went down, he gave me a showy slap on the bottom with an accompanying chuckle. It was as if he were broadcasting to those we passed, that I was "his," that he owned me and could do whatever he liked to me anywhere at any time.

Furious at his presumptuous liberty taking, I turned around and spat at him, "You do that again and I will break your arm!" Taken aback, he looked disbelieving. Momentarily sheepish, he said nothing. My anger amazingly had sliced through his pretension. It felt good.

I couldn't imagine what he had been thinking. He and I had never done more than kiss ... and, in fact, not much of that. He was a terrible kisser! Our lips rarely met. He approached each kiss with a widely-open mouth as if he were gargling. Then there was his Gila-lizard-sized tongue trying to tickle my tonsils. No matter what, I was adamant that he, and other men, were not going to pull that derriére slapping, -patting, or -caressing stuff in public.

One Sunday he called in the morning to suggest I accompany him to his married sister's home for a visit. I had already resigned from Sunshine Dairy because I was leaving soon so he knew I was possibly available. But the connotations for meeting his family were too intimate and committed. I said, "No." We argued. He pressed. I said, "No," again. And he pressed some more. He acted as if I had to have a "good reason," to say "no" and he was the one to determine if my reason were "good enough" for him to accept it—which, of course, it never could be.

Finally giving in, I kicked myself for doing it. As much as I wanted to be, I wasn't very good at standing my ground in general social situations with men. I knew I wasn't "allowed" to do so. It was obvious that I had to stop procrastinating and drop him soon. I only wished I knew a good way to do it so I would not feel guilty. I always felt guilty. Wasn't I ever allowed not to feel guilty about doing what *I* wanted to do in these situations?

When Marion, his sister, opened the door, she looked aghast. Of medium height and still carrying some weight from her latest pregnancy, she was in her faded blue terry-cloth bathrobe. With her uncombed, dark blond hair, she looked harried and not the least bit prepared for guests ... at this hour ... on a Sunday. There was no question I was intruding. It was, perhaps, one thing for Matthew to simply drop by unannounced, but it was quite another thing for him to bring a stranger, especially a female ... and on a weekend morning early. I was embarrassed for both Marion and me. Matthew, however, seemed oblivious.

From the appearance of the kitchen where she led us to sit down on plastic-seated, chrome dinette chairs she was in the process of laundering the diapers of the baby and the one-year-old. Last night's and this morning's dishes were soaking in soap suds in the sink. On the kitchen table beside the unfolded Sunday *Boston Globe* was a soft cloth and a bottle of liquid Pledge. An unplugged vacuum cleaner and dry mop stood nearby as if their use were already on her long to-do list. A baby's bottle rested in a pan of water being heated on the stove. She offered us coffee over the squalling of the baby in the next room where the one-year old was already demanding attention.

I empathized with Marion. She looked tired. I could see she was juggling and dancing as fast as she could while desperately needing a good night's sleep and a little help. What she was trying to accomplish was no easy task, though I doubted that Matthew appreciated it—not if he was traipsing through her early morning with a stranger in tow. We were the last thing she needed with her Sunday a.m. coffee.

As Matthew regaled me with the joys of parenthood in front of Marion, my synapses shouted at me in recognition that what I had feared was the reason he had brought me here. His not-so-thinly-veiled purpose was to extol the "fabulous benefits" and "satisfaction" of being married and having children. He wanted to show me that even with the household in a state of disarray, everything was wonderful. It reminded me of all the love-solves-everything endings of 1940's romantic movies, before reality sets in. This made me even more ill at ease. I glanced at Marion. She didn't look all that persuaded by Matthew's speech as she waited patiently, but pleasantly, for us to leave so she could start her chores.

Matthew continued, "Look at all the love that Marion and Hal have. Look at their wonderful home together and their great family life." Grabbing my hand, he pulled me along into the room down the hall to the right where the baby was in its crib crying loudly. His brother was jumping up and down, thunderously rattling the composition bottom of his playpen beside the crib. He looked to be in the process of deciding whether or not to join in vocally with his sibling's clamorous cacophony.

Matthew said, "Aren't those kids adorable? I just love them to pieces. I come here whenever I can to play with them. I love being an uncle. I can't wait to be a dad, to have my own." My ears rang from the noise and my stomach juices were turbulently rising into my esophagus, burning the tissue in their path.

Going back into the kitchen, I saw Marion form a tight smile. A real person, a wife and mother, she was anything but the propagandized picture of the 1950's ideal of deliriously happy wife and mother that Matthew, and many of the men I had encountered, still held dear ... and expected. She was not coiffed and dressed to the teeth with high heels and pearls, as if she had stepped out of a band box, something like June Cleaver on *Leave It to Beaver*. She was not floating ethereally from laundry hamper to cooking a French gourmet meal, greeting her husband at the door at night with a beatific smile, kiss, and a two-olive martini in hand, with his angelic children already having been quietly tucked into their beds so he could indulgently kiss their foreheads good night. Marion's life was not my vision of my future. I didn't appreciate Matthew's proselytizing, trying hard to get me to convert to his marital religion.

As we drove away, Matthew couldn't seem to stop listing his perceived benefits of marriage and kids. It was as if he wanted to make doubly sure I had absorbed his all-too-unmistakable message. When he finally paused for a breath, I interjected, "I hope you get what you want some day. I don't expect to marry for a long time. I'm really looking forward to heading to Baylor in a couple of weeks to start my pre-med program."

"Why do you want to be a doctor?" he asked. This was the first time he had broached the subject of my leaving this way. "You know women aren't respected as doctors. You could never be a neurologist. Operating rooms are like men's locker rooms. No women allowed except nurses, who are really subservient men in white dresses. If you became a doctor, you'd have to be a pediatrician. But you don't have to go all the way to Texas. You could stay here and go to college ... if you still wanted." I ignored him. This was to become a constant refrain for the short time remaining.

As my leaving approached more quickly, he began calling me daily, wanting me to go out with him. He was no longer a little clinging, he was suffocating. But how was I to tell him good-bye without bruising his ego?

From years of indoctrination by my father, and indirectly by my mother, family sitcoms, magazine articles, and advertising, I believed women were supposed to abide by a code which dictated that we should be very careful never to hurt a man's "vulnerable ego" That made zero sense to me. On the one hand, the culture proclaimed that men were such towers of strength, capable of leaping tall buildings in a single bound, and the *only* ones who could protect, preserve us and our country, and make *important* decisions for the world in war and peace. But, on the other hand, a female, but *not* another male, had to be super-careful how she trod because of his "tender" ego?

The following Sunday he wanted to take me to Medway where he and Charles used to ride. There was no getting around it. This was the day I had to end it with Matthew. I had no doubt he was preparing to ask me to marry him. If only I could have said good-bye over the phone, I thought. But my father had nixed that, pointing out, "That would be cowardly and not polite." My father had me well-trained about what "polite young ladies" did and didn't do. I always felt conflicted about what I "should" do versus what I wanted to do. So I reluctantly agreed I would tough it out somehow in person. Little did I know that this would shortly become a non-issue.

The country side was lovely with meadows and hills of green, broad-leafed grass, enclosed by split-rail fences.

Clusters of daisies sprang up all along the edges of the two-lane road. There was a large patch of grass nearby that had been newly-mown. It left the air still smelling of its crisp, stringent freshness, a scent I had always loved.

The weathered barn, still bearing traces of red paint from years gone by, was where the horses were stabled. It was close to the right side of the road and on the downhill side of it. I could see bales of straw for bedding and hay for the horses' feed through the barn's open double-doors at this end. I was hoping to spot some horses. Having had horses as a child, I loved to be around them. I loved their strength, independence, grace, and gentleness. No horses seemed to be present, either in the barn or in the nearby pasture.

Just then Matthew shouted, chuckling loudly, "Watch this!"

He stepped on the accelerator. The car sped up. He twisted the wheel sharply to the left. I slid across the car's gray plastic-covered front bench seat ... and fell roughly against him. It was from that vantage point that I could see what had happened. A black cat was scrambling for its life. The cat had come out of the barn and was crossing the road in front of us. Laughing like a maniac, Matthew was trying to run it down!

I grabbed the wheel, jerked it hard to the right. Shouting at the top of my lungs, I exploded, "What's the matter with you? Are you insane? That was so cruel! You could have killed that cat! How could you do such a stinking, lousy thing?"

He was still gasping for air in his hilarity. "Well, I didn't hit it, did I," he protested self-righteously.

"You were trying and would have hit it if I hadn't yanked the wheel from you. I can't believe you did that. What's the matter with you! Poor cat! You must have scared it nearly to death. At least it's still alive, no thanks to you!"

"You're making too much of it. It was just a cat. Besides, it was a joke. Don't you have a sense of humor?"

"'Just a cat'?" My voice rose an octave as my vocal cords tightened. Anger surged through my body, pushing out the veins on the sides of my neck. My face, throat, and upper chest tinted with spreading crimson. Hurt or kill an animal "a joke"? I loved, respected, and protected animals. I was always giving aid where necessary, whether it was to a rattlesnake caught in chicken wire fence surrounding our flower garden or to a crow my father had shot in the wing with a .38. And this person thought it was "funny" to scare, hurt, or kill one?

My muscles tensed, readying themselves for action. I wanted to wipe that smarmy smirk off his face with a punch that would require major surgical facial reconstruction. What kind of person would do such a thing? What did it say about him? He was definitely not someone I could ever respect ... or even want to know.

Although I regained some of my external composure, I retained all of my fury. Amazed, I suddenly realized that Matthew had, through his menacing behavior, solved my problem. That grotesquely negative and dramatic incident had finally *allowed* me to do what I had felt inadequate to do otherwise. We drove back in silence. The sun was dashing from twilight's third base and sliding into night's home plate, scoring a run.

As we now sat parked in his car in my parent's driveway on Dover Road in Millis, we had our last conversation. He started to plead with urgency in his voice, "But I don't want you to go. You don't need to become a doctor. You don't need to go away to college. Stay here with me. I want to marry you. I love you."

I set my jaw and chose my words carefully. No matter how I phrased it, I knew he would choose to misunderstand me. But I really didn't care. "I have already made my plans. I'm going to Baylor to become a doctor."

"I knew you weren't really serious about that. I knew you'd change your mind. I thought you loved me too. What about our future together? How can you go?"

Attracting and Dating the Wrong Men?

"Matthew, I do not love you. I have never said I loved you. I do not want to marry you. We have no future together. I'm going away to college ... period!"

He grabbed my wrist, "But you will love me. You just have to give it time. Don't go. I love you. You have to be mine. I need you." Minutes passed as he continued but it was all noise like the deafening drone of a turbojet engine. As I disengaged his grip and gathered my things together from the front seat to leave, he squeezed his face together as if he were going to cry. But his eyes remained dry. His voice became resolute.

"If you don't marry me, I'm going to join the Army. You are forcing me to do this. You'll be sorry when I'm shipped off to Vietnam because I could get killed or seriously wounded. This will be on your head and ... on your head alone." On that manipulative note, we parted company ... forever. He didn't call so I didn't have to refuse to talk with him.

However, after I arrived at Baylor, I received a letter from Matthew. In teary, passion-filled paragraphs he blamed me for his immediately joining the military. "You have ruined my life. If only you had said 'yes.' If only you hadn't run away and dealt with our love ... and life together ... like an adult, instead of a petulant child. Our life would have been wonderful. We'd have been like Hal and Marion."

The picture of Marion I had indelibly etched on my brain pan was of her dragging herself around the house, trying to keep up with all her "fabulous" duties as a homemaker and mother, despite her brother's insensitivity. For good or ill, she had made her decisions and I had made mine.

He finished his several-page, handwritten epistle by telling me he was severely depressed. The Army was "too uniform, compulsory, and authoritarian." He didn't know how much longer he could take it. "Life is no longer worth living. At least they issued me a rifle." With this gun he was seriously thinking of killing himself, he said, because, "I don't want to be here and wouldn't have been here if it hadn't been for you.

You've ruined my life." His vengeful parting shot across my bow was once again, "I hope your conscience will be plagued by my tragic, senseless death for the rest of your life."

I shook my head. His game-playing had persevered to the bitter end. Ironically, it occurred to me that my marrying him was what really would have plagued my conscience for the rest of my life. As perverse as it sounded, in retrospect I couldn't have been more pleased that he tried to kill that cat, but, of course, hadn't actually succeeded in doing so. It revealed to me how totally self-absorbed, manipulative, and soulless he was.

* *

Resulting Awareness: Always fighting for my recognition were several competing truths: My father was always in my head, telling me what I should and shouldn't do, what I should and shouldn't feel. But the compulsion of these well-learned tenets frequently conflicted with what my intuition and rational brain were telling me to do. This was the first time that I saw that I was being buffeted about by the expectations of others (my father and other males) which I knew did not work for me. I wanted to be assertive, but felt inadequate to be assertive. However, I discovered that when I became angry, all expectation bets were off. My heightened sense of injustice superseded everything else.

The question I asked myself: Why had the presence of strong negative emotion given me permission to override my previous training and how I could harness and positively use that again?

* * *

Texas

4

STEVE

Two months after I had arrived at Baylor, the Kingston Trio was to give a concert on campus. It was on one of their national tours. I was a great fan of their calypso-folk style even though I had none of their albums. Previously there had been a shakeup in the group. Because of differences about group leadership and music selection, Dave Guard resigned the original lineup in 1961, leaving Nick Reynolds and Bob Shane. They, in turn, had recruited their newest member and Guard's replacement, John Stewart. As much as I wanted to go, I couldn't afford a ticket.

Most of the time I was dead broke, except for the small pittance I received for staffing my dorm's switchboard. Back in Millis, my family was in significant debt due to my father's emotional problems and unemployment situation. So when Steve, also a brand-new freshman, asked me to go, I said "yes." However, I felt somewhat guilty agreeing to accompany him to the concert because I would not likely have accepted a regular date invitation from him under other circumstances. But perhaps it didn't really matter if we both had a good time.

Very tall, thin, with a long nose, prominent upper incisors, canines, and cheek bones, skin that had been pitted and discolored by acne, and gangly limbs, he was a jock. The few jocks I had met at Baylor seemed to me to be lucky to be at college, being there more for their athletic abilities than their SAT scores, though that may have been an unfair assessment. Baylor students adored and reveled in their football. Since I wasn't a football fan, was academically inclined, and in a time-consuming pre-med program, I found little of interest to discuss with them.

The Baylor Bears football team was a famous member of the Southwest Conference and had been a big winner years earlier. "Sic 'em, Bears." But now, in the early 1960s, they were virtually winless. As a result, Baylor acquired John Hill Westbrook who became the first African-American to play varsity football in the Southwest Conference. I found that move striking and very paradoxical. While I was there, the university had invited the classical pianist André Watts to perform in concert. However, that invitation did not extend to allowing him to use any of the rehearsal rooms in which to practice ... because he was Black.

Apparently the administration—which did not as yet admit Black students—and its White student body could ignore their prejudices *only if* doing so resulted in winning at football, but not for much else. And in fact Westbrook participated in the Baylor opening game of 1966 when the Bears upset Syracuse on national television. I felt ashamed that they weren't ashamed of their actions, especially since they loudly and often proclaimed being such "loving, tolerant Christians."

Since 1915, the Baylor Bears always had had a bear as mascot. It lived on campus in its own stark concrete pit of a home. It was taken on a leash to all the games. When I was there, I "met" Barney who was their current, aging mascot. I always felt bad for animals who were mascots, but especially for these large animals that needed a huge territory to roam in order to be psychologically healthy. As I watched him repeatedly walk the outermost boundaries of his pit, I saw what looked like the stereotypical behavior of a neurotic wild animal held captive in a small area. I had seen a polar bear in its cage do that for hours on end at Benson's Wild Animal Farm in New Hampshire. It seemed cruel no matter how well it might have been fed or attended to.

The evening of the concert, Steve arrived at my dorm bearing a large gold spider chrysanthemum to wear on my shoulder. These fall flowers were associated with the Baylor Homecoming Day and Parade and the Baylor Bears' football games. As considerate as his buying it was, the corsage seemed out of place for the concert. Irrespective, I wore it proudly for him which made him beam all over and even made his six-foot-plus stature seem more erect.

Oddly, the residence at which Steve picked me up had not as yet been given a formal name. But since it was a new hall, they conveniently referred to it "New Hall." Years later the large brick, three-story building was re-named the North Russell Hall and a corresponding mirror-image dormitory added to its rear became South Russell Hall. Since it was a long walk from New Hall to Roxy Grove Hall where the concert hall was being held, Steve drove us in his car down South 5th Street and right onto Speight Avenue. Because of the concert's sold-out attendance, we had to park a block away.

Steve looked neat in his pressed chinos and white, short-sleeve cotton shirt. I thought, however, he could have removed his green and gold Baylor beanie, emblazoned on the front with his year of graduation. These caps had been given to all the freshmen (and -women) to wear all the time during initiation to show we were "frosh." Mine resided on my desk at the foot of my built-in bed in my dorm room, never having been worn.

The concert hall was packed. Enthusiastic applause and cheering assaulted the trio every time they played and sang one of their all-time hits. The audience went crazy when the trio introduced their newly released, "Green Back Dollar." Their zeal was contagious. I was having a fun time. Except for his trying to hold my hand once during the concert, Steve was on his very best behavior. Wearing a perpetual smile, he appeared to be particularly pleased to have me as his date.

After the concert, he wanted to take me to a beer bust. If I had known what that really meant geographically, I would have made a pit stop at the concert hall before leaving. But not recognizing that Southern Baptists didn't drink alcoholic beverages, and certainly not on a Southern Baptist campus, I had made the invalid assumption the party would be at one of the athletes' dorms, like Penland, just a few streets away.

Instead we drove out into the countryside where there was a small grassy area, overlooking the city, surrounded on three sides by trees and scrub. All around there were numerous large wooden kegs of beer, each with a spigot in its bunghole, inviting a line of thirsty young men to partake of its contents. A single red and white cooler for soft drinks was to the side, open, and filled with ice and a few bottles of soda.

There was also "entertainment" (a term I use advisedly) present for the party. It was a three-piece African-American band which played and sang loudly mind-numbingly raunchy, tuneless songs. And the more raunchy, loud, and tuneless the song was, the more the Baylor boys present were screaming and laughing in hysterics. Some were dizzily dancing, followed by vomiting onto the grass before grabbing another white Styrofoam cup of brew. The girls present were sticking to the soft drinks so far as I could tell. Consequently, they weren't shouting, whooping it up, or hurling in congruence with the boys. One guy, who was barely able to stand, staggered over to a beer barrel and, with some semblance of coordination, managed to place himself on his back on the beer-sodden ground. His head under the beer spigot, he urged someone—anyone—to turn it on. Steve, foam cup in hand, was chugalugging and laughing along with the rest of them.

Nature was calling urgently to me by now. I asked Steve, "Do they have any facilities around here? I have to go."

"You'll have to go behind a tree." He pointed over his shoulder toward a mixture of live oak and locust trees, sagebrush, and silvery-blue winged saltbushes. Then he went back to howling at his cohorts who were sloshing their beer on themselves as they shimmied, bumped, and grinded.

Staring dispiritedly at the minimal cover presented me by the foliage, I could picture myself hiking up my skirt, then pulling down my panty hose and underpants, squatting, and trying not to soak myself, my skirt, and my shoes in the process ... all the while keeping an eye out for straying beer drinkers seeking a little sloppy action. As I began my search for adequate camouflage, I ran into another young woman who was coming from the trees.

"Did you find a reasonable spot?"

"As reasonable as it could be. Do you have a tissue with you?"

"Oh, right. Thanks," as I pawed through my purse for a fresh one.

I wandered quite far from the goings on before I felt comfortable enough to risk dropping my drawers in public. In the process I managed to sprinkle my shoes and snag my nylons on some saltbush spines but at least my bladder was happy once again. With myself pulled up, tucked in, and smoothed down again, I looked for Steve. The daylight was dwindling fast. He was well-entrenched in the general mood of alcoholic gaiety.

"Steve, I'm sorry but I don't feel well. I think it must have been something I ate for early dinner. Would you mind terribly taking me back to the dorm? You can come right back."

"Of course, sure. You know," he paused, reflecting, his eyes glazing over, "I think I know what you mean about dinner. I had something too that made me feel a little sick."

I smiled at that. We eased our way through the tight crush and he drove me back to my dorm. Somehow he did it without swerving out of his lane, running up onto the sidewalk, or clipping pedestrians in the crosswalks.

"Thanks so much for the concert, the lovely corsage, and the opportunity to meet some of your new friends. It was fun. Now you go on back and have a blast at your beer bust."

He made a deep bow from the waist to give me a chaste kiss on the cheek then smiled a beery little smile. He looked glad he had had the opportunity to show me off as his girlfriend for the afternoon then stumbled back to his car. The fun of the concert aside, I was glad to be where there were toilets with doors and people weren't puking on your shoes.

* *

Resulting Awareness: I learned that attraction and dating did not have to go together. I could go out with a man as a one-time thing just to have fun with no strings attached. Furthermore, he did not have to fit any "ideal" of looks or interests in order for me to go out with him. As a result, I found I could be a bit more tolerant—less judgmental—about whatever group he belonged to for this single activity. While I felt I still had to uphold expectation of myself as the "perfect young woman," I found once again the pressure of those expectations was less than when I had a romantic interest in the date.

The question I asked myself: To what degree did my degree of attraction to a male influence my allegiance to my gender-role expectations?

* * *

5

ROBERT AND RICHARD

It was a late Saturday afternoon in late October on the quiet Baylor campus. Elsewhere in the world Premier Khrushchev had sent a letter to President Kennedy regarding the U.S. military blockade of Cuban waters and air space so the Soviets couldn't deliver any more offensive weapons. The Premier had labeled it as an act of aggression, further ratcheting up the Cuban Missile Crisis. Ironically, only a few days later when Kennedy *would* have received the letter, the Waco City emergency sirens went off accidentally around ten in the evening. Panic and chaos ensued. My dorm mates were racing about. Removing their window screens, some climbed out to find their boyfriends for a last, or first, fling before Armageddon. Others crowded into the dorm lounge to pray together to ask God not to let the Soviet Union nuke us. I hung by the radio instead to see if I could learn what was going on.

But as of this Saturday, well before this letter was to be received by Washington, I was in my dorm room on the first floor, wondering where everyone was and what they were doing. An hour earlier I had already finished my scheduled time at the dormitory switchboard for which I received fifty cents an hour. I was unenthusiastically preparing to plow through biology and chemistry books for courses. Still amazed and happy I had made it here, I was attempting to contend long-distance with the serious problems at home in

Massachusetts, where my father was still jobless, currently physically ill, and we were losing both our car and house.

Carol, who lived down the hall but was acting as residence monitor today, knocked on my door. "There are two guys from Connally Air Force Base, that Cynthia knows, on the dorm phone who are looking for Coke dates. How about it? Are you up for it? Everyone else seems to be out already."

I was wearing a large gray, no-name sweatshirt which hung down to my thighs, my underpants, bra, and my sneakers. "Do you know these guys?"

"No, but Cynthia is supposed to know them." I didn't know Cynthia well but hoped that if she, as a "strict Southern Baptist in good standing, had approved them, they were likely as not to be okay.

"I guess. Things have been pretty dead lately." I was envisioning two young men with perfect posture, all spit and polish. "They're from the Air Force base, huh? Yeah. That would be okay."

"There are two of them so we need to find somebody else as well."

"Delphie is doing pretty much what I was going to do this evening. I'll see if I can get her to go. We could use a break."

Delphie was from Elgin, Texas, pre-med, and a whiz in the inorganic chemistry lab. She was a brunette who eschewed makeup, with a full figure, and a rowdy sense of humor. I got such a chuckle out of how she said, "yes." It was as if it were "yaahss" which she would exaggerate just to get me giggling.

That afternoon we had had a nearly lethal laugh when someone in the chemistry lab had somehow mixed potassium permanganate crystals with concentrated hydrochloric acid. Suddenly the room was cloaked in a dense yellow, lung-searing, choking cloud. It was World War I all over again. We were being gassed with chlorine. Flinging open all the doors and turning on the exhaust fans, we all raced outside. When Delphie and I finally stopped coughing and crying, we started to guffaw about how dangerous pre-med could be. We could laugh at most of the absurdities of life which seemed to abound in a college environment. She was a great, committed lab partner and a fun friend.

"They'll park out front and one of them will let you know they're here."

James T. Connally AFB was seven miles northeast of Waco on Airbase Road. Whenever there were functions on the base, a bunch of us non-Baptist women headed on over via transportation provided by the base. Only we "heathens," as we were sometimes referred to by our religious female cohorts, went because Baptist women didn't dance, or play cards, or, allegedly, do much else. In addition to being labeled a heathen, I was also considered a "hippie" because I used to wear stockings with clean, white sneakers to class as part of my casual attire. Most of the other young women wore rolled down heavy, white athletic socks and black suede loafers. I even saw some wear them with cocktail dresses to administrative functions. At the base they played records so the guys could dance and have some female companionship without having to go off-base. It was all very "regulation."

Up until the time I was in Waco, the base had trained instructor pilots from many allied nations and already-rated pilots as bombardiers and navigators to provide triple-rated crews for B-47s. As I understood it, that was discontinued in 1962. They then provided Undergraduate Nav Training until 1966.

Delphie, who was also up to her elbows in biology and chemistry notes, was glad to get away from studying for a while. We both dressed in skirts, blouses, stockings, and flats. I put my hair in a long pony tail. After announcing to Carol, who was stationed at the el-shaped information desk in the public lounge, that we were ready for our expected guests, we waited on one of the bright orange sofas there. The front area of the lounge was all-glass. I didn't like the idea of going on a blind date but thought I could try it just once. At six on the dot a middle-aged, slightly balding man walked up the few front steps leading to the dorm, through the tall, square concrete pillars at the front and glass double doors, and walked forward to the monitor's desk to inquire about us.

He looked okay. In fact he wasn't bad looking, a little like David Janssen, but somehow he didn't appear to be Air Force style. He looked slightly paunchy around the middle, perhaps because he was slouching. His clothes, which didn't look as snappy as I expected, at least seemed to have encountered an electric iron in the recent past. His overall self-presentation struck me as out of sync with the Air Force. But what did I know? I'd only seen the younger guys from Connally so far. And they had been into the spiffing Captain America fly-boy image.

"Hi, I'm Robert. We're out front. Richard is in the car. Nice new building you have."

Delphie and I smiled, introduced ourselves, and walked with Robert out to his unpolished, dark blue 1960 Chevy. His blond, curly-haired friend was sitting in the front seat. Richard slowly unfolded himself onto the curb. He must have been six-three or -four. With angular facial planes like Clint Eastwood's, he wasn't bad looking. But when he smiled, I gasped. My stomach flipped. His teeth appeared to be covered in moss.

That set my early radar-warning system shrieking. There was no way green teeth were allowed in the Air Force. But what was I going to do now? I felt stymied. Should I ask to see their AFB identification? I didn't want to create a scene. I was always afraid of creating an awkward situation even when I *knew* I should do something *other* than what I was about to do. I swallowed my reservations and injudiciously entered the car.

I sat beside Robert in the front seat which left Delphie with Richard in back. I didn't know if Delphie had as yet noticed Richard's algae crop. She gave no sign of having seen it but she was often pre-occupied with chemistry problems.

"Where are we going?" I asked, thinking we were likely going into Waco. When I first arrived at Baylor, Waco had been a culture shock. I didn't quite know what to make of its famous large rotating neon cross rising skyward from a nearby church. While it was a city, I had seen men strutting around in cowboy boots, fancy-stitched and otherwise, with high heels that made them walk with their butts out, something like women in their high heels. I had seen fancy western shirts and ten-gallon hats, though many business men wore their cowboy hats with their suits. Men seemed to wear their cowboy hats everywhere. Surprisingly, I didn't see them take them off in restaurants or other places indoors, except in church.

Baylor students, on the other hand, did not appear in any such attire in public that I ever saw, except in costume on a Homecoming Day's parade float or in a stage performance. Instead they looked "collegiate," right out of the Conservative's Guide for Appropriate Young Adult Christian Attire. Baylor was not a place for anything outside the "clean-cut 1950s' norm."

My hope was that we were headed into Waco because if anything went awry, Delphie and I wouldn't be too far from campus to hike back a mile or so. However, that hope was destroyed when Robert said, "There's a roadhouse just out on Route 77, a little south of here. We go there a lot, don't we, Richard."

Hearing this, I wanted to go into full-blown denial. I felt I had mucked up royally not pulling Delphie aside, pointing out Richard's oral hygiene problem, questioning if he could really be Air Force, and then getting her take on what we should do as a result. Delphie had no inkling of my concerns which I should have shared.

"Yeah," Richard piped up with a snort from the back seat.

"So, Robert," I said, "what is it you do at the base?"

"I'm a mechanic."

"What do you work on? Cars or planes? Or both?" He didn't respond. I wanted him to prove me wrong, that maybe he was on the base even if Richard wasn't.

The area through which we were now passing was wooded with live oak and ash. It seemed we had been driving for quite awhile when we came to a wide, weathered-gray roadhouse on the left side of the road. Its unpainted wood looked to have been sand-blasted by years of heavy Texas, grit-laden winds. There was a tall, sizzling pink neon sign out front with part of the name extinguished, leaving only "ack's Sh t." Two cars were parked in the gravel lot near the entrance. To my surprise when Robert pulled in, he drove his car way over to the left side and stopped toward the rear of the building. This struck me as being unnecessarily out of the way. It also required us to walk lots farther to the front entrance on the larger pieces of shifting gravel.

We entered into a large, rustic room with lots of small round tables and chairs hugging the perimeter so people could dance in the center on the tiny dance floor. Decorated with all sorts of cowboy paraphernalia, it boasted two fancy, highly-polished Western saddles which were draped over sawhorses. A stuffed buffalo head on a walnut-stained wooden plaque greeted us as we entered. On the unpainted walls were spurs with fancy rowels, coiled bullwhips, colorful horse blankets, chaps, and saddlebags. There were even several sun-dried, white skulls of deceased steers, like those made famous by Georgia O'Keeffe in paintings of New Mexico. In spite of this

Attracting and Dating the Wrong Men?

welcoming Texas ambiance, there were very few warm bodies around. The jukebox was playing some sad country-western song where the singer's sweetheart had been killed and he was seeking revenge, probably with his shotgun at the ready. Robert moved our party toward the back to find a round table for four which was in an alcove off to the right. Delphie and I sat side by side across from Robert and Richard.

Robert took Delphie's and my orders for Dr. Peppers and Richard's for bourbon, then left the room. Dr. Pepper was all the rage at Baylor at the time though I found the red, fruity soft drink to be too sweet. It had actually been invented in Waco in 1885 by a young pharmacist named Charles Aderton who worked at Morrison's Old Corner Drug Store. He had originally named the concoction a "Waco." When the drug store couldn't manufacture enough to meet the demand, The Circle "A" Ginger Ale Company took over manufacture, later becoming the Dr Pepper Company. At Baylor it was even served hot in the cold months with a slice of lemon at the Student Union. Robert returned shortly with our bottled sodas and straws.

"Robert, you were telling me you're a mechanic. What do you work on at the base?"

Robert and Richard exchanged knowing glances. "Well," Robert began tentatively, looking down before continuing. "We don't actually work on the base. We just said that."

Oh, crap! I thought. I really didn't want my fears confirmed. Ignoring and suppressing them was easier. "Do you really know Cynthia? You were supposed to be friends with her."

"Well, no. When I called, someone asked if I were friends with Cynthia. I said 'yes,' thinking it might grease the skids a little. We called hoping a couple of you college girls might come on out with us tonight."

He had Delphie's attention now. She and I swallowed hard and quickly looked sideways at one another. The person who answered the phone had automatically asked if they were friends of Cynthia? Talk about a careless move. It was almost as dumb as my not trying to check with Cynthia first about these guys. She might have been around. I felt stupid and vulnerable.

Just then someone blew in on us like a tornado. It was a dark-haired woman of medium height in faded jeans and a short-sleeved print top. She tapped Robert on the shoulder. She whispered something into his ear. He got up silently. They left together. Delphie and I looked at each other, eyes wide. We were stunned. What was going on here? Shortly she returned ... alone. This time she told Richard to leave, which he did.

When both men were gone, she looked us up and down, appraising our attire and manner, and she asked, "Who are you girls?"

With my heart in my mouth, I spoke up first, "We're from Baylor. We were asked if we wanted to have a soda with two guys from the Air Force base. We were told they were known to one of our dorm mates so we accepted."

She visibly sighed, "I'm sorry to have to tell you girls this. These two are married ... and ... they don't work at the base."

We both paled. Delphie looked as if she had been slapped in the face. I thought, and they're married too? Who was this invading stranger? Before she could utter another syllable, words tumbled breathlessly out of my mouth, "We're so sorry. Honestly we had no idea. Please forgive us."

The middle-aged woman with a soft nasal twang and prematurely lined, sun-broiled face continued, "I'm Robert's wife." My saliva dried up instantly. My heart was tripping. My eyes searched for an exit other than the front door behind her. She remained standing, looking directly at us, and continued,

"This is not the first time he has done this sort of thing. However," she paused, "I'm here for another reason." It was getting worse by the minute. Delphie and I held our collective breath. "Richard's wife is very jealous of anyone even looking at Richard."

In the back of my mind I couldn't help wanting to snicker at the ludicrousness of anyone wanting to kiss Richard. But there was no question Robert's wife was deadly serious. My facetious thoughts dissolved instantaneously.

"Richard plays around a lot and she knows it."

Increasing fear was percolating to the surface. Remaining controlled, Delphie and I waited silently for the other shoe to drop. It was going to make an ugly thunk.

"She's on her way over here ... right now ... and she's carrying a large knife! She always carries that knife. She called me, very upset, to tell me that she knew Richard was stepping out on her ... again. She knew he'd be here because he and Robert always come here. You girls are not safe."

Delphie's tongue apparently had stuck to the roof of her mouth because she couldn't seem to utter a word, emitting only a guttural sound from way down in her throat. This was a dire situation. I managed to secrete enough moisture into my mouth to start to speak, "I can't tell you how sorry—how terrible we feel about this mess. We need to call a taxi right away because we don't have transportation back to the dorm."

I had no idea if there were a taxi service available out here, wherever we were. I had no idea what a taxi would cost. I had only a few bucks with me from my switchboard paycheck and had no idea what Delphie was carrying in her handbag.

"I'll drive you back to campus."

"We don't want to put you out any further." Delphie poked me hard in the ribs with her knuckle to shut me up. I could read Delphie's thoughts loud and clear: Richard's knife-wielding wife is about to arrive and you want to wait for a taxi?

Are you out of your mind? We could be bloody cadavers lying on the unfinished hardwood floor before a taxi arrived.

"Girls, Sarah will be here shortly. It's not safe for you to wait for a taxi. I'll drive you."

I was both glad and scared. Robert's wife may not have been as calm as she seemed to be. Maybe she had had enough of Robert's gadding about and would do us in inside her car ... just because. It didn't matter. We had no choice. Richard's emotionally-unbalanced wife wasn't going to take out her anger on her beloved Richard. Instead she would target those college girls who were "attempting to seduce him and lead him astray." Waiting for a taxi was a really lousy idea.

Robert's wife's dust-covered, old green and white Ford was in front of the door, unlocked. There was no sign of Robert or Richard. She hurried us out. Delphie and I hustled into the backseat. Revving it up to sixty, she peeled out of the parking lot. A cascade of pebbles rained behind her. We roared north on Route 77. In all honesty, I was glad to be on the road again. If our driver were planning to do us in, we would deal with it later.

As she drove, she started a conversation, asking us what we were studying, how long we had been at Baylor, and if we liked it. I wondered if she had ever had the chance to go to college, some place where she could have expanded her horizons f she had chosen. She came across as intelligent, assertive, with common sense and a good grip on reality, despite her hanging on to a gallivanting cad like Robert. I hoped he had some redeeming qualities. She was also good in a crisis, for which I was supremely grateful.

Once we started to respond, Delphie and I kept up the flow, both of us being careful to avoid asking her any personal questions. We were definitely heading toward Waco and campus. This was a good sign and some hitherto quiescent part of me wanted to cheer out loud. Maybe we would make it back unscathed. Maybe there would be no need for Tex Ritter to sing "Blood on the Saddle" at our piggybacked funerals.

To my delight she found New Hall with little difficulty. As she parked in front of the building, she leaned over the front seat back, arms firmly planted on it. Sternly she imparted some motherly words of caution to us, "You girls have to be more careful. You seem like nice girls and I wouldn't want to see you hurt. This could have been ugly ... very ugly ... and it very nearly was. In the future you need to know *for sure* who your dates are."

Through the car's open back door we thanked her profusely for her incredible kindness. As Delphie and I raced to the dorm door, I wondered about Sarah, her mental state, and her seemingly odd relationship with Richard. But not any of that mattered except for Robert's wife's caring admonition.

I didn't know what Delphie did when she reached her room—I never asked her—but I ran as soon as I could to the shower. I felt so dirty. No matter how much I scrubbed my body, I couldn't wash away the memory of what had happened ... and what very nearly had happened. If I didn't want a repetition of this evening's situation, I couldn't be so unassertive. I needed to feel confident enough to find out what was what before hand. But I hesitated. Could I *really*? Suddenly Scarlett O'Hara came to mind as she put everything aside, "Tomorrow is another day." For the moment I was just glad to be alive.

* *

Resulting Awareness: Quickly I discovered that safety is an important issue because men can lie to get what they want. This was my first in-your-face experience with that. This does not mean you should be paranoid, but it's essential to have a sense that things are truly what they appear to be. And if you check and discover that they aren't, you need to feel justified and be willing to act on that knowledge. But because I lived in fear of negative evaluation and rejection, I never felt I had permission to question a man or any authority figure about anything. This was even when my gut and brain were shouting at me to do something different. I had been shot down by my father too many times for trying to do it. Bucking the expectations' system was a dangerous thing to do.

The question I asked myself: What had I ever done in opposition to my father's forbiddances that felt good both in doing it and afterward—something I could repeat?

* * *

Massachusetts

6

EDDIE

For obvious financial reasons I returned to Massachusetts after only one year in Texas, moved back in with my parents who were now in South Natick, found a job, and immediately enrolled at Framingham State College. I wanted to pick up needed science courses on the off-chance I could get into another pre-med program. The reality was that there were always exponentially more applicants than openings in the few actual pre-med programs around Massachusetts at that time, such as at the University of Massachusetts at Dartmouth.

While at FSC, I became friends with a middle-aged woman going for her Bachelor's Degree in English. She worked part-time at WKOX radio station in Framingham. The station was located on 100 Mt. Wayte Avenue, about two miles from the college, down and off Franklin Street. She had a weekly ethnic community program. Spending time with her at the station on Sunday, I was learning the rudiments of radio production which I was exploring primarily for fun. She even let me read announcements occasionally. Before and after her show, I had a chance to meet the various members of the WKOX family—announcers, broadcasters, sound technicians, the program manager, and interns.

There was one older man named Eddie who showed some interest in me. Saying he was "older" was being charitable. He was, in fact, only a few years younger than my father as I uncomfortably later discovered. This was a fact which didn't please my father, especially when Eddie addressed my father as "Dad" when he met him. Broadcasting local and state sports and related events, he was known widely for it, especially his football play-by-play.

Heavy-set, of medium height, with brown eyes, a warm smile, and light brown hair, his voice was what held appeal for me. Its mellifluous tones soothingly enveloped my ears. When he said he wanted to phone me occasionally to chat, it seemed harmless enough. Since he didn't ask for a date, I agreed. I've always been a sucker for voices, like that of Don Wescott, the voice talent who later was the twenty-year voice of PBS programs, such as *Nova*, before Will Lyman took over as narrator.

Soon, however, Eddie wanted to talk more frequently ... and then "go out." I wasn't interested in him and didn't have the time anyway. I was trying to cram in as many courses per semester as possible, mostly at night. This meant I spent most of my time studying when not managing a bookshop part-time at Shoppers World in Framingham. As I soon discovered, "going out" and "dating" were not synonymous in Eddie's vocabulary. "Dating," in the traditional sense of going somewhere and doing something together to share an interest in it, was not what he was about. Instead, his thing was to sit in his old, black Ford sedan and talk and talk and talk. Saying Eddie was tight with his money was like saying a person about to give birth was "a little bit pregnant." Divorced, he guarded his money obsessively, living in a small, 1948 silver Airstream travel trailer.

Very quickly Eddie's topic of non-stop conversation became laser-focused and single-minded. With great fanfare, he introduced me to his grandiose proposal for what he was going to do in his next career. It would, as he repeatedly told me, "kick a goal in the last second of the game to win the championship." Furthermore, he said, "Radio program managers and my listening audience will be so amazed that they won't know what hit them!" His big dream was to ditch his sports' broadcasting—the only subject he knew, as it turned out and for which he had a huge audience—to have his own personal-development and motivation radio program.

Specifically, he wanted to emulate Earl Nightingale, the internationally-known motivational speaker, author, and "Dean of Personal Development"—to be, in essence, "Earl Nightingale Junior." While he had as yet done nothing to test his proposal's practicality and marketability, he spoke of it as a *fait accompli*. He informed me, "It will be a smash hit, taking off like a rocket, making me a household name!"

Unfortunately, it wasn't long before it was obvious this was only a daydream. It was an abstract idea stuck in neutral that never shifted into first-gear because it remained totally lacking any realistic details, research, methodology, or plan structure. Moreover, it had several glaring problems that would need to be resolved before he could even create a preliminary plan to test.

His entire career to date had been based on sports, knowing football and ice hockey backwards, forwards, and inside out. He hadn't a clue what "personal development and motivation" was. As opposed to applying Nightingale's concept to sports, he wanted to do the *exact* show Nightingale already did with Nightingale-like stories and Nightingale-like quotations. Constantly reading to me from Nightingale's books, he seemed to believe that bathing himself in Nightingale would confer upon him an understanding of the underlying psychological principles as well as the skills necessary to apply them.

Whenever we spoke, he eagerly rehashed his dream. There was something child-like about it. However, what would have been appealing in a ten-year-old looking into his or her adult future was less than attractive in a man in his early forties who was about to chuck everything for something about which he knew absolutely nothing. One evening feeling truly battle-fatigued from feigning interest in his continuous monologue, I decided to offer what I considered a potentially helpful comment. I did it when we were once again sitting in his old clunker in my parents' driveway. We were always in his car because I was *not* going to go to his trailer as he repeatedly requested. Little did I know what was about to befall me as a result of my making a comment.

"Since you're an experienced and talented sports broadcaster, have lots of local and state recognition for your work and a large sports audience, I was thinking you might consider making this Nightingale program your own by using a sports' angle. Something similar to Nightingale's present show but about personal development and motivation *as it pertains to sports*."

The look on Eddie's face was one of horror. It was as if I had zapped him in the bahdoobies with a cattle prod. Visible in the light from my parents' dining room window, his features ran the gamut from shock to pain to outrage. I felt as if he saw me as an enemy combatant intent on torturing him where he lay helpless in the mud by shoving the butt of my M-16 into the gaping bullet hole in his leg. He was absolutely thunderstruck that I would *dare* to comment, make a suggestion, offer an opinion, or even remotely question him about what he wanted to do.

Rage was visibly building as he glowered, asking in a strangled voice, "Can you possibly be suggesting ... I can't do it? How dare you suggest such a thing! Just who do you think you are? What do you know? You know nothing! I'm the radio professional! I'm the one people listen to. I'm the one with the voice—the one that people clamor for!"

I was flabbergasted at his response. Maybe I had phrased it inadequately. I certainly didn't say he couldn't do it. As a friend, I had thought what I offered might give him something to think about for executing his proposal. Naïvely I then tried to clarify what I was intending to communicate. "I'm not saying I doubt you can pull off creating your own show. But since Nightingale is internationally known, syndicated, and has best-selling books and tapes available everywhere, and since you already have an enthusiastic, well-established audience, maybe you could aim your Nightingale-like program at them." That apparently didn't work any better. His look was murderous.

Knowing I had to stop, I didn't want to. I was tired of keeping my mouth shut, deferring to males and their opinions irrespective of their irrationality or lack of validity. But I forced myself to let go. He was determined to misunderstand me. Every word I uttered was making it worse.

His facial muscles dropped as if weighted down with hate. His eyes narrowed to slits below his furrowed brow. Astonishingly his lower lip also protruded as if in response to a crushing disappointment, with tear glands at the ready, "You know absolutely nothing about radio or what radio listeners want." His voice cracked. "*I* know radio. *I* know my audience. They love me. They want me." He was not only blind with anger but also with petulance. Furthermore, he was totally ignoring the fact that he had just supported what I had suggested about playing to his existing sports-loving audience.

The situation was as if I had accidentally stepped in pile of dog feces. With my every attempt to extricate my shoe I was sinking in deeper. He looked hard, even more insulted and no less hostile. Leaning across the car and me, he opened my door and visually pushed me out into my parents' yard without a word. I imagined that meant I was rid of him. Relieved, I felt I now wouldn't have to find a way to tell him good-bye which I had been contemplating for some time.

Unexpectedly, after a brief hiatus, he called, appearing to having "forgiven" me for my "misstep." Despite my annoyance with his outrage at my speaking out, I saw him a full week later. Why couldn't I just say "no" and have the courage to cut the umbilical cord? When we were together, I was bored insensate, saying "uh-huh," carefully avoiding agreeing or disagreeing with him about how he was going to "rule the airwaves."

One evening the next week things suddenly changed. As we were sitting in his car in my parents' driveway, Eddie said, "Let's get married." My mouth dropped open. Shock consumed me. I could not have heard him right. Maybe he said, "The Mets get carried." Could this be coming from the same person who felt I had committed the most grievous of sins against him? My mind couldn't seem to disentangle the threads of this psychedelic crazy quilt. He was suggesting I marry him but with the unspoken proviso that I keep my opinions to myself?

Without skipping a beat, he continued, revealing "our future." "We will live in my little trailer until those great things happen for me. I can feel that they are just around the next corner, waiting for me. It will be my big break. We will hit the big time *together*!"

Once I untied my tongue, I reminded him, "We're friends, nothing more. I do not want to marry you."

At that he reached over and grabbed both my arms. He began to kiss me hard, pinning my back to the seat upright, as if to discount and dismiss my statements by shutting off my words with his lips. I wrestled to free myself, thinking "Get your damned paws off me." That show of disrespect made me angry. But he was going to do whatever he wanted irrespective of how I felt about it.

The next thing I knew he suddenly shoved my left hand onto his sweaty crotch where he was fully erect. I was resisting. Vehemently I said, "No!" Holding me against my will, but particularly for something sexual, was intolerable. "No!" I wanted to shout as loudly as possible but was afraid my father would hear and come out. That would have been too embarrassing. Moreover, I'd have been labeled "at fault." As I struggled with his strong grip, he rhythmically moved my hand back and forth. "NO!" He ejaculated. His brown polyester pants became soaked and smelling of mangoes. I wanted to wretch.

I was so livid I had to scramble for the words to express myself. "Eddie, when I say 'no,' I mean 'no.' Your using force is totally unacceptable. I don't care how you think you feel about me. I do *not* want to see you again." On that note, I departed the car immediately.

Shortly thereafter, Eddie called to ask if I'd do one *last* thing—go to an awards dinner with him. He explained he was to be receiving some community recognition for his sports broadcasting work. The way he described it, sounding disconsolate, he didn't want to go without a date at his table, someone to cheer for him and look proud of his accomplishment. I didn't want to go but felt bad about him sitting all alone at his table at what I was sure he considered a "momentous" occasion. "Okay, I'll do this as a favor, but this is absolutely the last time we see each other." If only I had had the intestinal fortitude to have said "no."

To my surprise, when we arrived at his table in the local restaurant chosen for the ceremony, his two brothers and their wives were there, waiting for him. He wouldn't have been alone. He already had his claque there to root him on. Was it just that he didn't want to be seen without a "date"? Or … was it something more … as my gut doing flip-flops was predicting?

As our rubber chicken dinner was being served, conversation was somewhat stilted with a palpable strain. I couldn't discern its cause. I wondered if he had told them of his marriage proposal and my refusal. Something was in the wind and it wasn't blowing anything good my way. If I had had my own car with me, that would have been an excellent time to simply leave.

After eating, Eddie excused himself. I thought he was heading to the restroom, but then he didn't return. From the moment he left it took no time for things to circle the bowl. Both his brothers and their wives showed by their body language they were prepared for something, no doubt at Eddie's bidding. Little did I suspect what was about to happen.

It seemed that Eddie had complained to them that I was "evil incarnate," that I was stomping on his radio show dream with football cleats. He was desperate for their help to right this indescribably unforgivable wrong. I felt like Alice meeting the Jabberwock on the field of battle without my vorpal sword in hand.

First his brothers took turns like a wrestling tag team, "How dare you tell Eddie that he can't do the show he wants to do. Just who do you think you are? He knows what he's doing. You don't. You know nothing. You're bringing him down. He has lost his confidence. You have no right to try to destroy this man's dreams." I sat there mute, uncomprehending. On and on Eddie's words came out of their mouths as if they'd carefully scripted and rehearsed this dramatic soap opera scene.

Then the men, apparently having shot their wad of curare-tipped darts, got up from the table together. Eddie had still not returned. Looking satisfied, the brothers likewise left, handing over the reins of their vitriol to their wives who took them up with undeniable relish. Eschewing darts, these women used rotisserie skewers. Their faces twisted in a religious fury, they snarled at me, "Just who do you think you are? Girlfriends and wives do not do that. You have no right, no right at all. It's unseemly. It's inappropriate. It's un-Christian. Eddie doesn't deserve such vicious, rotten behavior from you. You're a castrating bitch of Satan and you need to know your place!"

Attracting and Dating the Wrong Men?

I managed to get a word in edgewise, "Wait a minute. I'm not his girlfriend or wife and I didn't say anything 'un-Christian' to him!"

"We know exactly what vile, disgusting, venomous things you said to him."

"No, I don't think you do. I told him—"

"You're a soul-murdering Jezebel! You just don't get it, do you? You have *no* right to criticize him. He knows what he is doing. He's the one who knows about the radio business. You know nothing about it! It is not your place to make comments about his plans. It is not your place to make suggestions to him about what he does or should do. It is definitely not your place to question *anything* he does or wants to do. He is the one to make these decisions. You have no right to try to destroy his precious dreams. So keep your big fat wicked mouth shut!" They then resumed their pre-dinner demeanor as if the director had called, "Cut!"

On cue, the men returned with Eddie. Their wives looked up at them with the slightest of satisfied smiles. Insulted and outraged, I didn't know what to do as they all resettled themselves at the table, exchanging meaningful glances. Impotently I envisioned them suffering execution by the mythical red-hot poker method attributed to effecting the death of England's Edward the Second in 1327. I wanted to tell them what to do with themselves, leave the table, and call a cab. But I didn't have the money for a cab with me for that distance. And I certainly wasn't going to argue with the religiously super-self-righteous, especially being outnumbered five to one. So I sat there stewing in my powerlessness. All that now remained was for Eddie to receive his recognition. They cheered him. I contributed some weak applause, unimpeded by any enthusiasm.

Unbeknownst to him, Eddie was going to hear about what he had wrought whether he liked it or not. Feeling supremely justified in my anger, I was not about to let what happened at dinner go unaddressed. All the way home, I seethed. When we arrived at my parents' house and he had turned off the engine, I looked directly at him, and said, "Your behavior is reprehensible. You ran to your brothers and their wives like a little child with some tale about my being a big, bad, despicable person because I offered you a simple comment on your proposal. Then you had the unmitigated gall to have them viciously attack me for you. Just who do you think you are to think you can treat me that way and get away with it? Actions have consequences."

"You don't understand. Girlfriends and wives are loyal. They don't interfere with a man's dreams. They don't murder his hope. You said my dream was no good. They support their man no matter what he does."

"You are so full of it! Never ... ever ... contact me again."

I reached for the door handle, opened the door, and slid through before he could say anything further or try to grab my arm again for more involuntary sexual activity. Once inside the house, from the dining room window I could see Eddie still sitting behind the wheel, looking nonplussed. He didn't seem to comprehend that this woman—"Satan's spawn"—would act that way toward him. Dictating to him? Women weren't allowed to do that ... and certainly not to him. He had thought his brothers and sisters-in-law would have straightened me out about that ... that they would have put the fear of God into me. But it hadn't worked! Suddenly he backed out of my parents' driveway fast. I wondered if his religiously-patriarchal philosophy about women was why he was divorced.

A letter followed to give me a "second chance to come to my senses and reconsider the huge mistake I was making." He emphasized he was "still willing to marry me." I shook my head and marveled at how truly "Christian," merciful, and self-sacrificing he undoubtedly thought he was being. What a jerk! A few futile calls found me unwilling to talk to him other than "hello" and "good-bye." He finally gave up. Sadly, I suspected there were still women, like his sisters-in-law, who might be more accepting of his dictatorial expectations. If so, I wished them lots of luck. They would need it. However, as I discovered online decades later, his big dream never even made it out of the realm of wishful thinking and he never remarried.

* *

Resulting Awareness: Eddie initially felt like a surrogate for my father because of his age, authority status, and his gender-role expectations of me. I found it particularly difficult to assert myself because in the back of my unconscious, I was forbidden to do so. Consequently, I let myself be controlled and treated badly. I had allowed myself to become Eddie's psychological victim, as I was with my father.

The question I asked myself: What did I get out of following males' gender-role expectations of me and what could I do to make me feel better about myself irrespective of their expectations?

* * *

7

PHIL

If such things had been considered for the *Guinness Book of World Records*, I would have been listed for having the periods of three women at once. Super-tampons? I used them two at a time and still had to change them often. This particular night I was packed to the gunnels to guarantee protection. Being the equivalent of a belt-and-suspenders person in this situation, I also wore dark reddish-brown faux suede slacks hoping I could camouflage any minor accident should it occur. My evening counseling group session was at Framingham State College on the second floor of Dwight Hall. Since medicine still hadn't worked out, I had taken degrees in psychology with emphasis on interpersonal communication as a backup. The students and I were seated in a circle on curved cream-colored institutional chairs with stainless steel legs. Totally engaged, we were discussing ways to share in group, how to avoid attacks on others, and how to deal with conflicts between members.

By an ominous pricking in my thumbs I knew something was wrong, that I had better high-tail it to the nearest restroom. I gave instructions to the students, "Please practice what we have covered about how to respond to clients' angry and critical statements. I'll be right back."

Down the hall in the restroom, leaning against the gray steel stall wall, I saw how inadequate "Super" could be. The tampon maker had shouted to the rooftops that "each tampon could hold a cup of liquid." This was obviously an exaggeration since I had been wearing two with a sanitary pad and was totally drenched, from groin to knee. Moreover, there was no doubt that I hadn't carried the overflow with me. Wrinkling my face as if smelling Limburger cheese, I knew my chair was still being occupied by me in my absence.

After I cleaned myself as well as I could, freshly re-stuffed myself, and layered inches of paper towel in my wet underpants, I grabbed a dozen of the cheap, brown, folded recycled paper, some of which I wetted, and headed back to the classroom. The students were immersed in their practice as I re-entered. With distaste, I approached my chair and saw the extent of the mess. Using every paper towel I had at my disposal, I mopped, wiped up, and cleaned up as best I could what was now a red congealing pool.

No one said anything as they tried to keep focused on their task at hand, despite my chair being right in front of them. Men and women alike looked discomfited but vaguely sympathetic to my plight. Perhaps their being psychology students helped a little so they didn't run screaming from the premises. However, I could hear the men thinking, "Oh, that is too gross! I didn't need to know about that." And I could hear the women thinking, "Thank God that didn't happen to me! I would have died of embarrassment."

There was no question that I needed to bathe and change my clothes now. Waiting for the ninety-minute class to end was unacceptable from a visual, olfactory, and tactile standpoint. As I searched the students' faces to see whom I should choose as a replacement for me, I calmly explained, "As you can see, I've had an accident. I'm going to have one of you takeover for me for the remainder of this class. Everything will be okay and we'll have our class at our next regularly-scheduled meeting time on Thursday. In the meantime, Beatrice, would you take my notes and lead the class in these other exercises." She nodded okay. "Thank you." I was amazed at how collected I sounded as I spoke with them despite the unmistakable squishing between my legs.

I had to call Phil, my new boyfriend, to pick me up early. We had planned to go out to grab a quick bite after my class tonight so I hadn't driven. How was I going to handle this? Even though I was in a state of uncomfortable, sticky sogginess, and none too happy about it, I didn't want to elucidate to someone new in my life about my private-soon-to-be-public accident. That seemed too tacky.

Men, as a general rule, aren't particularly entranced by the messiness of a woman's period. And a new significant other especially tends not to want to think about such things as he's following his step-by-step fantasy seduction plan with you. I knew I'd have to tell him flat out, have him take me home, and then decide from there. There wasn't much choice.

Expecting yourself to be the "perfect" date collides with your being human. Doing what you think you're supposed to do and being what you think you're expected to be doesn't necessarily work out in dating, or in anything else for that matter. I said aloud to myself, "If Phil's repulsed by it, then that's life." I suddenly remembered a dorm mate from Baylor who had a similarly embarrassing situation with which to deal.

Connie who was a tall, slim blonde with shoulder-length, naturally curly hair was very religious and very concerned about acting properly and in accordance with the social and religious dictates of what women "should" do. She and Todd had been dating regularly since they were freshmen. Everyone knew they were an item and expected them to marry soon after graduation, in a few months, even though neither Connie nor Todd talked much about their marriage plans to friends.

They did everything together from watching Baylor Bears football games, singing in the Baylor choir, attending church, listening to the radio, taking Bible study classes to collecting food and clothes for the poor in Waco. Of course, they did not play cards or dance or drink or engage in premarital sex because those activities were prohibited by their Baptist teachings by which they strictly abided, or so they said.

On this particular Saturday they had been together for hours before the sun trailed off into the west. Earlier they had dropped off canned goods at the food bank, watched some Little League play, and wandered around the furniture shops in Waco picking out fantasy bedroom and living room suites. Then they had stopped by the local college hangout for burgers and fries in a bed of shredded lettuce in a red plastic woven basket and shared a Coke.

It was a sultry evening in Waco. As usual, Connie was dressed in a knee-length print cotton skirt, white blouse with a Peter Pan collar, rolled down white athletic socks, and black suede loafers. Todd was in his collegiate best with chinos, tieless light blue short-sleeve shirt, and blue blazer. However, despite Connie's conservative concern, he allowed himself one small nod to non-conservative dress, especially in warmer weather. That nod was his open-weave, leather-strip huaraches he wore with navy socks. While he liked that his feet could breathe, he was adamantly against the sandals that hippies wore, as well as against the hippies themselves across the country.

As they walked back toward the campus, they passed a Gene Ewing's Camp Meeting, a "deliverance tent revival" in full-swing. They had been to it a day earlier so knew the evangelistic preacher would be raising the dead. When they had attended, some non-believers from the college had disrupted the evening by chuckling behind their hand-covered mouths as a person in a white sheet wearing a small golden crown rose from the coffin and then skipped in behind the preacher's pulpit. To Connie and Todd it felt so disrespectful.

"Didn't those people know how they were supposed to act at a tent meeting, especially when the preacher was raising the dead? This was a religious service after all."

This time they were too busy looking into each other's eyes and clasping each other's hand to attend. They kept walking. Soon overhead the well-known rotating neon cross revealed itself, bathing them with bluish light as they passed. Two doves—though they might have been pigeons—swooped in front of them which they took as a positive sign from God.

One of the things Connie believed was that she needed to rise above her humanness. That meant she would try her utmost not to cough, sneeze, blow her nose, or do anything that took away from the expectation of her feminine perfection, especially in front of Todd whom she looked to and respected as her soon-to-be "lord and master."

But by the end of the evening Connie, who had avoided using a public ladies' room during their time together because she considered it unacceptable, was beginning to dance from one foot to the other. This was even as Todd held her close for kiss after kiss. Kissing was considered PDA, "public display of affection," and frowned upon by Baylor powers that be. But since no one could see them in the deepening shadows in front of New Hall, they enveloped themselves in each other's arms.

However, the pressure on her bladder was increasing. In pain as her sense of urgency heightened, Connie really needed to get inside to the nearest restroom. Totally unaware, Todd didn't want to let her go and held her even more firmly in his strong arms. "I'm sorry, Todd, but I need to get inside before they lock the front door." He nuzzled her neck, whispering he could unlatch her ground floor window screen for her. She made up an excuse, "My roommate needs my English notes right now for the upcoming test."

"Okay, in a moment, please," he squeezed her tight and continued with kiss after kiss. She started to pull away from him and back toward the door but he drew her to him once again, "Please, just a little longer." As sweet as he was, as tender as his embrace was, as much as he loved Connie, nothing now could prevent the inevitable. Connie's burgeoning bladder succumbed to the emergency. Urine cascaded down her legs, into her socks and shoes, onto Todd's chinos, and into his sandals, soaking his socks and breathing toes.

Connie was mortified. Todd released her immediately, shocked. Unable to utter a sound, she raced inside her dorm, assured she had destroyed her image of female date perfection and ruined her relationship with Todd ... and with any other man who heard about her disgusting, animalistic behavior. However, to her unalloyed amazement, the next week Todd formally asked her to marry him and they set a date for right after graduation. While she had said "yes," she felt thoroughly confused by his actions since she had so publicly disgraced herself.

It could turn out okay for me too, I thought. I finally affirmed my decision to go ahead and tell Phil the truth and let him decide what he wanted to do. As a result, I sat on his *Boston Globe* as he dropped me at my apartment in Framingham so I could clean up. He then picked up Chinese/Polynesian take-out from the Moon Palace so we could eat a leisurely meal. What happened after that, however, did not turn out so sanguinely.

Because I continued to have these untidy accidents, my doctor referred me to a gynecologist at Brigham and Woman's Hospital in Boston for a D&C, dilation and curettage. After having read Robin Cook's *Coma*, wherein twenty-three-year-old Nancy Greeley goes into the hospital for a D&C and leaves brain dead as a result of a so-called "anesthesia complication," I was concerned about general anesthesia. General anesthesia or heavy sedation was pro forma for the procedure at the time. So when I discovered from the gynecologist's office I wasn't going to have either, I was glad it would be a local anesthetic instead. However, at the same time, I didn't know how well local anesthesia could work. Was it like the nerve root being totally numbed for dental work? I didn't question it ...and I should have.

The gynecologist was a somewhat gruff older man with graying hair and wire-rim glasses. I met him when I was already positioned on the uncomfortable exam table in his office suite, with my heels in stirrups, and a nurse at my side. I've never felt Emily Post would have approved of my shaking hands between my spread legs like that. I know I didn't approve. But I did it to make the point that it was impolite for him not to meet me first when I was still dressed.

Stating, "This won't hurt a bit. It will feel like a pin prick," he went straight to work injecting my cervix with Lidocaine or some other deadening agent. My God! Pin prick, my butt! We were talking pain! What he no doubt meant, of course, was "You're a female. Females can tolerate giving birth to babies. You can handle this."

After a few minutes, when he had determined I *should* be numb, he inserted something like a miniature version of the speculum, which was already providing access to my vagina for his manipulations, to stretch my tiny cervical opening. That really hurt. But that was nothing compared with his inserting a metal rod with a sharp loop on the end into my uterus ... and scraping my *un-anesthetized* tissue. The pain was blindingly exquisite. If I hadn't felt I had to use all my willpower to keep from screaming at the top of my lungs, I could have stood up in the stirrups and slugged him with extraordinary-adrenaline-infused strength, sending him staggering across the room.

If he had been an Inquisitor, I would have confessed to anything—to assassinating President Kennedy or being responsible for the Red Sox continuing to lose the World Series from 1918 to 2004—to get him to stop. My whole body tensed in response to each movement of the razor-sharp loop.

But he continued to dig all around and scoop out the overgrown layers of cells. I wanted to shout, "Where is that damned anesthetic? It's NOT in my uterus!" This was insanity. I could see why this was done under general anesthesia. It was too painful and dangerous to be done any other way. This was purest torture.

The piercing, spasmodic pain festered itself in anxiety that caused me to increasingly tense the muscles of my abdomen, pelvis, and thighs. He raised his voice, "Relax!" Then speaking brusquely, his voice rising in volume, he said, "I can't do this when you tense your muscles. Re-lax!" And just how did he propose I do that? Totally lacking empathy, he was not timid about expressing his frustration and anger with me, which, likewise, did *not* help me relax. His attitude—echoing that of other male physicians I had experienced—was one reason I had determined years ago that whenever humanly possible I would have a female gynecologist ... no ifs, ands, or buts.

I tried my best to relax but anticipating every excruciatingly sharp tissue shave locked my muscles in even more tightly. I felt I was being rasped, harrowed, excavated, and gouged out like a badger's burrow. What made it worse was my knowing that my skyrocketing muscle tension increased the likelihood of his actually perforating my uterus, resulting in my probable bleeding to death. Later physicians determined that using this metal loop for a D&C was too dangerous. It was replaced by a vacuum procedure. That didn't help me in my current circumstance, however.

In lieu of giving me a shot of bourbon and a bullet to bite down on, his nurse suggested I squeeze her hand when I was tense or felt the pain. *When?!* Poor benighted angel of mercy didn't know what she was suggesting. My response to the convulsing pain gave me the strength of ten. I squeezed her hand so tightly I kept waiting for its small bones to crackle and crumble as I heard her knuckles grind together. Did she truly believe this was going to compensate for the torment of having a rat ferociously gnawing at my innards? At one point she seemed to struggle to disengage my hand. I was sure it was because blood had literally ceased to flow into her white, cold fingers. "Forget it, sweetheart," I thought. "What I'd rather be grabbing and squeezing I can't reach," and continued to hang on for dear life.

Afterward, as I bled for a short while but didn't exsanguinate, he resumed his professional composure and returned to being Dr. Jekyll. His eyes telegraphed to me that he was not pleased with having had to deal with a "hysterical woman." To keep me from ovulating for six months so I wouldn't build up more tissue in need of scraping he recommended he surgically implant Depo-Provera sticks under the skin in my upper underarm ... without anesthesia, no doubt.

That was not acceptable. I had researched Depo-Provera because of court-imposed implantations of it in women who had been found guilty of abusing their children. It was like temporary sterilization, invasively preventing them from becoming pregnant again. There could be resulting medical problems from implantation.

"No thanks," I said. "What if I have a reaction to it or experience an overdose? What would I do then? I would have to have someone surgically open up my arm to remove them to deal with it. No, I'd prefer to have something I can take daily, that I can have some control over."

Once again he showed his extreme displeasure with me. But this time it was not for "non-compliance" but rather for my having the insolence to question his medical expertise and recommendation. Face darkening, he grudgingly gave me a prescription for a progesterone medication to be taken by mouth daily and sent me on my way, no doubt hoping I didn't darken his door again. Shortly thereafter, pathology confirmed the diagnosis of *endometrial hyperplasia*, a proliferation of cells from a possible chronic inflammatory response, hormonal dysfunction, or compensation for damage or disease elsewhere. My pre-existing painful polycystic ovary syndrome could well have been a hormonal contributor.

While the tissue sample indicated that no cancer cells were present, the tissue itself posed a significant risk factor for endometrial cancer. This meant I had to continue to monitor it carefully. But, I vowed, not with him ... and *never* again without some sort of twilight sleep at the very minimum. Afterward, I still had intermittent bleeding episodes and an occasional accident. That plus my occasional bouts with gut-grabbing pelvic pain which interfered with our joint activities finally sent Phil off to greener pastures. It was an unattractive and inconvenient problem that took the bloom off the dating rose all too quickly.

* *

Resulting Awareness: This was my first realization that I could rise above gender-role expectations and my unconscious allegiance to my father and my mother's behavior. I stood up to the doctor which felt wonderful. Furthermore, I could see myself stepping into more independence, listening to my rationality and intuition and acting on them instead of on others' expectations of me. I saw that even though I had compared myself to Connie, I wasn't Connie. I felt stronger and freer to be more assertive even though I was not totally beyond feeling I had to moderate that assertiveness on occasion, whether I liked it or not.

The question I asked myself: How could I nurture and further reinforce those expressions of assertiveness so I was less likely to regress into unassertiveness?

* * *

8

BENNY

After Framingham, I had moved to Wellesley. Most of my time was now spent writing and teaching but I made sure I took time to paint and sketch outdoors. There was something in the way the early morning light hit a wet canvas ... or the wisp of lilac, lily of the valley, or rose fragrance floating in the air ... that stirred my creative juices.

I was ensconced on the shoreline of Lake Waban, my favorite painting spot. A tickling breeze under-sided leaves with a slight swish and playfully nudged the water. It made a nearly silent lap against the pebbles at the lake's edge. Such tranquility nourished my mind, body, and soul. This use of my leisure time had become like a religion to me. I always came away from it inspired, revived, and energized, ready to tackle my tasks once again with renewed vigor.

This April was rapidly becoming the loveliest I had seen in years with green sprigs slipping through the thawing soil everywhere and crocus showing their purple and golden heads earlier than usual. I had just cemented my easel in the softening earth at the edge of the lake at its closest proximity to Pond Road which connected Routes 135 and 16, the two main drags through Wellesley.

This road was the western boundary of the five-hundred-acre Wellesley College, the private women's liberal-arts college which had been founded n 1870. A member of the original "Seven Sisters Colleges," it is consistently ranked among the top ten liberal-arts colleges in the U.S. Landscaped by Frederick Law Olmstead, Jr., Boston's preeminent early-20th Century landscape architect, it is known for its picturesque beauty, including woodlands, open meadows, as well as Lake Waban.

Settling in, I had already spread out my paints, palette, palette knives, and brushes beneath my folding camp chair. I was working on an unfinished canvas, focusing on an eccentrically-inclined sycamore just around the curve of the shore. Hanging from it and partially submerged was a lightning-assaulted branch. Its smaller branches had created a small rock-and-leaf weir around which the water eddied. While I often worked on landscapes, I wasn't interested in photographic realism. Instead, I wanted to suggest shapes and color that evoked emotion and resonance to something universal.

Suddenly a deep voice shattered the stillness. It startled me, interrupting my visual concentration, "Hello!" I turned to see a tall, pale, thin figure in a dark sports coat, gray gabardine trousers, and white tieless shirt, walking toward me on Pond Road from the direction of Route 135 on the north. When he arrived, he stood by a small boulder near the road, behind me. My stomach lurched. Almost by reflex I quickly surveyed the area for any sign of traffic or the presence of others.

With a long-fingered hand he smoothed his rumpled hair. Its straight darkness accentuated his deep-set, forlorn-looking, blackish-brown eyes flanking his long, arrow-like nose. He smiled crookedly. His cheeks formed parentheses around his thin-lipped mouth. His sharp features were not unpleasant but his intrusion was. He had absconded with my sense of peace, leaving me disquieted. Trying to ignore him, I found being all alone with a strange man in an isolated location made it impossible for me to get back to my painting.

Within only seconds of his arrival, he asked, "Do you come here often?"

"No," I replied with an edge to my voice.

"I don't see a cooler," he stated, edging closer to incline his upper torso over my shoulder as if inspecting my work. I could feel his hot breath on my neck as he invaded my personal space.

Shivering, I said, "I'm not here that long. Please step back. I can't work with you leaning over me."

This was my time, my place, my meditation, and he was profaning it. I took a few moments to compose myself. Inhaling deeply, I set my jaw and turned around to ask for his silence. But he was already ten feet away, walking rapidly south down the road, toward Route 16. As he disappeared over the crest of the hill, I let out a great sigh of relief. I felt as if a leaden mantle had been lifted from my shoulders. Maybe I could get myself back in the mood to get the tree on canvas structurally. However, my gut was nixing that idea, spurring me to leave. Despite my feeling of unease, I wanted just a few more minutes to work on what I was doing so I ignored my unconscious warning.

Twenty minutes passed quickly as I was contemplating the peeling wood and bark around the broken limb. Suddenly a panting sound seemed to fill the air from the south. I could feel a cardiac palpitation. Trotting toward me was the man with the hound-dog eyes. He was carrying a medium-size, white plastic bag from the Wellesley Market.

"Stupid!" I muttered to myself.

"Hello again," he called, his cheeks red and wet, his hair flopping lankly on his brow. "Great artists have to eat, you know, to keep their creative juices flowing." He rummaged through the sack. "Tuna sandwich, Mountain Dew, and 'Nilla Wafers." He thrust half of the sandwich at me.

"Thanks," I said, glancing up at him for only a moment, "but I've already eaten."

"You're way too skinny. You need to be more—what do they call it—oh, yes, 'Rubenesque,'" he said enunciating each syllable as he tore a large chunk out of the mayonnaise-spread bread with his hand.

Rubenesque? I thought of the full-figured woman in Rubens' "Venus at the Mirror" with rolls and saddlebags clinging to her body. I mentally shook my head. As a runner, I was more athletically streamlined ... and preferred it.

He shoved the other half-sandwich toward me again which I rejected. "My name's Benny. Benny Lawson." He made a noise with his mouth as he suctioned tuna particles from between his teeth with his tongue and dislodged a piece of celery with his finger. "I'm a manufacturer's rep for sports equipment companies. I can get you basketballs, soccer balls, and protective gear wholesale. Interested?" He laughed again and stuffed the rest of the half-sandwich into his mouth.

I suppressed a shout of frustration. Tranquility, meditation, and inspiration were no longer within my grasp. They had been replaced by an odd sense of foreboding. I began disassembling my tubular steel easel and gathering all my gear. Benny's mouth ran non-stop except for his downing the Mountain Dew in a couple of gulps, and shoving a few Nabisco cookies into it. Distracted, I really wasn't listening ... until he began speaking about the dangers of being a woman alone.

"You know," he began, smiling, as I balanced my camp chair and canvas, "you really shouldn't be here all by yourself. It's a long, lonely stretch. Someone could be lurking behind a tree or a stone wall, watching, and waiting. Or arrive in a van to snatch you. No traffic. No police. It's not safe for a woman alone." He shook his head slowly and dramatically.

I shuddered as he continued, "I mean, what would you do if someone came after you? Call for help? No one could hear you ... not from across the lake or from Routes 135 or 16." I kept moving toward my car. "You would be totally at their mercy." He finished with a concerned smile, "But, seriously, you would be—are—at risk. I don't want to see you at risk."

Every square inch of my skin was crawling as if a webbed nest of gypsy moth caterpillars had dropped on me from the branches above. Anxiety was closing like a fist around my heart. Every nerve fiber was screaming at me to pitch everything and get away from him. I had no idea what his intent was but it felt as if he were a mortician sucking out my security and ease and replacing them with trepidation.

He paused. "What this means is," he said, suddenly morphing into a soothing Mr. Rogers, "you are in need of protection. And that's why I'm here. I'm here to protect you." He grinned again.

Was this some new pick-up line? He was defining the situation as one of risk then assuming the role of the one who would protect me from that risk. It reminded of what Jerry Rubin had said about definitions. Rubin had been a member of the Youth International Party (Yippies), a radically youth-oriented, counter-cultural off-shoot of the 1960s' free speech and anti-war movements, and later a well-known entrepreneur. He asserted that the one who has the power to define the situation has the ultimate power. That certainly seemed to be what Benny was attempting to demonstrate.

Then, he said, "Hey, let me help you with those." He grabbed at my easel and paint box as I was trying to juggle them with my canvas. Reaching my avocado green VW Rabbit which I had pulled well off the road across from my painting spot, amid the trees, he said, "This is why I stopped in the first place. When I saw an empty car on this secluded road, I thought there might be a damsel in distress—someone in need of my knightly, protective assistance. And, see, I was right." He smiled again.

Attracting and Dating the Wrong Men?

Creepiness was enveloping and chilling me. I unlocked the car, took the easel and paint box from Benny, and placed them with the canvas on the back seat, making sure nothing was touching the canvas which was still-tacky with thick oil paint. My plan had been not only to put in the broken branch but also to touch up the reflections of the leaf-filtered sunlight on the water. But I never had the chance. Paranoia which was now quietly bubbling to the surface made me wonder if I would have that chance again.

As I started to ease myself in behind the wheel, Benny already had his hand on the passenger side door handle. My anger and fear sprang forth as I wanted to shout, "Get your hand off my car door or else."

Before I could think of anything to say that was not antagonistic, he stated, "I hadn't planned to be here this long but with getting you lunch and then helping you with your gear, I'm late for a phone appointment. How about giving me a lift into town?"

Anger submerged my fear. I wanted to throw the car into gear, jam my foot on the gas, and leave him standing in my dust. But I also didn't want him angrily writing down my license number to track me down through the Department of Motor Vehicles. Perhaps if I gave him a lift, that would be the end of it. "Okay, where? I'm heading toward Bay State Road."

"Oh, that's fine. You can drop me off at the post office in Wellesley Hills." Once ensconced in my passenger seat, he began to hum all the way down Pond Road, left on Washington Street, and into Wellesley Hills. Occasionally he stared at me as if assessing and memorizing my profile. It was unnerving. Shivers intermittently scaled my vertebrae.

The post office was a short distance from a small farmers' market, purveyors of organic fresh vegetables, eggs, and milk for vegetarians and other health-conscious consumers. I went there a lot. I knew everyone by name and thought of them as friends, especially Alice in fresh produce.

She likewise was an old-movie buff. We were constantly playing a game of "Do you remember ..." about some movie scene, secondary actor, director, or bit of dialogue. Their store on Washington was about three-quarters of a mile from my home on Oakland Street which was near the Massachusetts Bay Community College.

As I dropped him off, I wondered how he happened to be at Lake Waban ostensibly without a car. He wasn't dressed for jogging. Had he been visiting one of the estate homes along the road behind their large wrought iron gates, high rock walls, and long driveways? And what was with his ominous scenario? While I had been going to that location on Lake Waban every Sunday, after that encounter it seemed more prudent to avoid that spot for at least a couple of weeks.

I had plenty of other things to do. I had one book out at that time. It was an alternative psychological approach to job hunting with emphasis on networking, having mentors, and personal marketing. Now I was working on my second which was about non-traditional, practical tools for career development. In addition, I wrote articles for the weekly newspaper, the *Wellesley Townsman,* and took freelance writing assignments, several of which were currently sitting on my desk anticipating completion.

With fanfare, the third Monday in April arrived. It was Patriots' Day which meant the running of the glorious Boston Marathon. Begun in 1897, it was the longest continuously running footrace in America. Twenty-six miles and three hundred eighty-five yards, the course strode from Hopkinton to Boston, covering Routes 135, 16, 30, and then onto Boston's city streets. It was run irrespective of the weather.

From my vantage point along Route 16 near my home, I cheered and applauded all runners and wheelchair participants, professional and amateur, just for having the determination to be in the race. Years later there was Dick Hoyt pushing his physically-disabled son, Rick, in his special race-designed wheelchair. They were to eventually participate in all sorts of events together, including triathlons and biking across the U.S., completing 3,735 miles in forty-five days, as well as surpassing one-thousand races. They continued to do so for years in an effort to help those physically disabled become active members of their community. Always of special recognition, Team Hoyt soon became a staple of the Boston Marathon. As a result, a statue in their honor was erected in Hopkinton in front of Center School at the starting point of the race. Their sailing by the crowds always elicited even louder cheers and more applause if that were possible.

Forever memorable was 1967 when Kathrine Switzer entered the race as "K.V. Switzer" when there was ban on female competitors. She was the first woman to run the race with a number: "261." Before her Bobbi Gibbs had run and finished unofficially for several years. What was particularly noteworthy was when Switzer and her boyfriend were running together, about two miles into the race, race official Jock Semple tried to rip off her race number and shove her off the course. Switzer's boyfriend grabbed Semple and threw him to the curb. Switzer finished the race. I loved it. Female runners were not formally admitted for another five years, but after they were, they made us all proud with their stellar athletic performances.

Always I came away from watching the race hoarse and with red, swollen hands. As a runner, I averaged about forty miles a week in the nearby neighborhoods. My hope was merely to finish the race some day. But to participate in the Boston Marathon with a number I had to qualify in some other marathon first. I never quite got that far.

By the time the following Sunday had rolled around, I needed a painting fix—that feeling of peace that composing and creating in communion with Nature gave me. Fantasizing that I could start on the branch at seven-thirty in the morning, I expected I could get in a half-hour in the crystalline morning light which super-saturated all the colors of the water, rocks, and foliage. I also wanted to finish the reflections on the water.

As thirty minutes ticked by, the cool crispness was disappearing. It was time to go. While quickly stowing my gear in the back of my car, I heard the irritatingly familiar voice swoop down on me, like an eagle zeroing in on a rabbit zigzagging through the tall grass. "I was wondering when you'd be back. I have something for you." Huffing and puffing, as he strode up the hill from Route 16, he handed me a small brown paper bag. "Open it."

"Wondering when I'd be back?" What was that supposed to mean? "That's kind of you but I don't accept gifts from strangers." No sooner had I said the "s" word, I bit my tongue.

"I'm not a stranger. How could we possibly be strangers after our last meeting? I'm your personal protector. Open it!" His smile was determined. Inside the Corkum's Hardware bag was an inexpensive squirrel hair brush.

"That's thoughtful of you but I really can't accept it." I didn't want to take anything from him and attempted to hand it back.

"Yes, you can! It's a small gift. I want you to have it," he pushed it back at me. My body felt a chill even as the sun rose. I took it with a soft "thank you." No matter how I might try to deny it, it was abundantly clear that I had to forsake Lake Waban's shore. I knew I couldn't finish the painting there. Once again he asked for a ride to the post office but in such a way as to assume it was automatically his. I reluctantly gave it to him, hoping this would be our very last encounter. I did not like his manipulations and ... I did not like him.

My budding paranoia and foreboding were wrestling for my attention. In their scuffle I recalled the 1960 *Twilight Zone* episode called "The Hitch-Hiker" where a young woman, played by Inger Stevens, is driving cross-country, from New York City to Los Angeles. Along the way from Pennsylvania on she keeps seeing the same man on the side of the road hitchhiking. Perhaps this was not my last encounter with Benny, *my* hitchhiker, irrespective of my no longer coming to Lake Waban.

As spring rolled into summer, I found I was frequently running into Benny or spotting him. This was ratcheting up both my fear and anger. When I went to the post office to mail a manuscript, he arrived for stamps. When I bought a seafood quiche for dinner at Captain Marden's on Linden Street, he came in looking for cod. When I was at the main library on Washington Street doing research, inside the farmers' market buying fresh broccoli, and at the Wellesley Recycling Center on Great Plains Avenue near the Needham line, I saw him. Sometimes he nodded but mostly he watched me with a slight smile without approaching. As annoyed as I was with his current surveillance of me, I was unprepared emotionally for its escalation.

Somehow he had gotten my number. He phoned me with suggestions for future newspaper stories, stories he said he knew would be really good for my reputation. I was stunned. I hadn't given him my name or number. Then it came to me. Of course, he had seen my photo and name with my newspaper articles. Even so, I certainly had not given him permission to call me.

"If you have article ideas, please mail them to me in care of the paper. Do not call me." Sounding hurt by my request, he said, "I was just trying to be helpful," and hung up. While I hoped he would get the message and leave me alone, my churning gut told me not to count on it, especially now that he knew who I was and where I lived.

I arranged to have my phone number unlisted. I was confident I wouldn't hear from him again, at least by phone.

To my chagrin my being "unavailable by phone" lasted for only twenty days. How he obtained my new number I didn't know. But now he was calling ostensibly to give me more suggestions though it felt more like he was checking up on me. It was harassment but what could I do about it? He wasn't threatening me.

As summer melded into September the calls had slowed to a trickle, and then only a drip, drip, drip. I suspected that was less about a reduction in his compulsion to call than about my complaining vociferously to the phone company that someone had given out my new unlisted numbers. I was grateful for the break and hoped it lasted. But this was not to be.

In the middle of the month I lay in bed incapacitated with pneumonia, feeling sorry for myself. In my fevered moments I blamed my weakened condition on Benny's continuously stressing of my immune system. Exhausted, at two a.m. I had just nodded off when the phone rang. It took four rings to penetrate my awareness. Drowsily I picked up the receiver, knocking the amber prescription vial of industrial-strength antibiotic on to the floor. There was a faint, plaintive cry, "Help. I've hurt myself. I'm bleeding."

"What?" I started to cough. "Benny? I have pneumonia. Call 911."

A prolonged, fading "please" came through then I heard the phone hit something hard, maybe a table or the floor.

"CALL 911!" I tried to raise my voice but started to cough heavily, requiring me to snatch my inhaler from my night table. When the sticky tickle eased off, I brought the phone to my ear. There were no further sounds but the line was still open. Putting the phone back on its cradle, I reluctantly threw back the covers and dropped my legs over the side of the bed. Slipping on my scuffs which lay beneath, I staggered out of bed to my office to grab the phone book. My whole body ached and begged for sleep. A "Benjamin N.

Attracting and Dating the Wrong Men?

Lawson" was listed at 005 Woodlawn Road. That was a short distance away.

"Should I call 911 to see if he's called?" I began a dialogue aloud with myself, "What would I say? 'There may be a serious problem but I'm not sure'? And what if there isn't? Maybe I should check it out and then call if necessary. What? Are you out of your ever-lovin' mind? You're sick ... really sick. If he can call me, he can call 911. Benny is not a puppy caught in a storm drain I truly have to rescue." Suffering from oxygen- and sleep deprivation, I wasn't thinking clearly. If I had been, I would have called the police, explained the situation, and stayed in bed. Then they could have been the ones to check it out.

Dizzily I dressed, in spite of my thinking better of it, pulling on a heavy-cotton, long-sleeve jersey and slacks, and my running shoes. Then I splashed my face with cold water to wake up. But my eyelids continued to droop. As I made my way to my car, which was parked in back of the small deep-yellow saltbox I rented, it started to rain. Cold drizzle slapped my face. I cursed myself now for not having brought a jacket with me. I couldn't figure out what I was doing putting myself at further risk in the cold wetness. Slowly my car wound down toward Washington and turned left on Woodlawn.

My lungs ached with the exertion of trying to breathe. My eyes kept closing. My head fell back then snapped forward again as I fought off sleep. I was an accident waiting to happen. In a long five minutes I was in front of a soon-to-be ramshackle, three-story house, replete with hints of incipient peeling ochre and dark green trim paint begging to be touched up, in stark contrast to the better-preserved New England-style homes around it. The trees still in full-leaf obscured the finished-attic apartment. At this hour in the rain in my condition I found it particularly loathsome. The mailbox said "Lawson #3."

The dark green front door squeaked on its hinges and groaned with the sound of melancholy in the dampness as I made my way inside. The hall and stairwell held tightly to the fusty smell of neglect. The whole area was badly lighted. I stumbled on the ragged, once-vibrant Oriental-designed stair tread as I slowly ascended. Every two steps I had to pause to catch my breath. My ribs were tightening around my lungs. I wanted to cough a deep cough from the bottom of my lungs but stifled the urge. Once it started, I knew I wouldn't be able to stop. I could see myself desperately gasping for breath, crumpling into a heap on these aged steps, perhaps not being found for days, having become food for maggots, cockroaches, and rats.

In the pre-dawn light of a forty-watt bulb on the third floor I found Benny's door. Wheezing, I knocked softly, not wanting to wake up anyone who lived on the second and first floors. No response. I knocked again. No sound. "Go home," I shouted to myself, "he's probably gone to the emergency room at Leonard Morse Hospital in Natick." As my last act before leaving, I tried the door knob. It turned and the door swung in slowly, opening two feet. "Benny?" I whispered as I pushed it far enough to see into the room. "Benny, are you here?"

Emerging from behind the door, a spectral Benny appeared. His face was the same color as the white bath towel he had wrapped around his hand. "I hoped but didn't dare to think you'd come," he said weakly.

"What happened?" I gasped for a breath. "Have you called 911?"

"I was opening a jar of pickles and the glass shattered." He looked as if he were a Southern lady about to swoon with the vapors and raised his swaddled hand with the other. "The blood ... the shock. I ... I couldn't ... handle it."

Swallowing a cough, I felt myself start to sweat. I wanted to lie down. I needed a portable oxygen unit. Anger was the only thing keeping me conscious. "Let me take a look at it." At this point, I didn't care if he had sliced an artery open from his wrist to his elbow. I unwound the towel with great care as I looked for pulsing fresh blood.

The last fold revealed two coagulated cuts on his thumb, each about an eighth-inch in length and superficial. "What? You got me out of my sick bed for this? For two lousy cuts! For godssake! I have pneumonia! When did this happen?" As my blood pressure rose, I was feeling less faint and finally started to cough.

"Around ten-thirty, I guess. I didn't have any gauze or tape and was afraid the cuts would open up again if I fell asleep."

I wanted to tell him to eat excrement and die. "Get me a clean handkerchief and some Bacitracin." Feeling what little energy I had drain away, I slipped to a sitting position on the arm of his faded floral sofa to the left of his front door. After he gathered the items together, I slathered the ointment on his "wounds" and wrapped the fabric around his thumb, tying the ends together. No wonder he hadn't called 911. He called me instead ... and, bloody hell, I came!

Benny was now lying on his sofa as if he had lost all his strength as a result of blood loss and the stress of his ordeal. "You've saved me," he mumbled in a voice that was barely audible. "Now you are my protector as much as I am yours." With that he rose haltingly to guide me into the dimly-lit hallway.

Before he closed the door, I moved my foot into the disappearing opening. With exertion I managed a breathy, "Get this straight. I am *not* your protector and you are *not* mine. You are NOT to call me ever again ... for ANY reason!" His mouth curved downward as his face took on a deeply-aggrieved expression. Removing my foot from his door, I hyperventilated as I dizzily made my way back to my car.

The inside of the windshield had fogged so badly I couldn't see out. Firing up the engine, I snatched up a role of paper towels I always carried on the backseat for emergencies and tried to remove the moisture. It would not yield to my importuning. My frustration building, my face contorted into a tear-soaked howl. I slammed my fists onto the steering wheel until a coughing jag overtook me. The heater slowly came on full-blast, having the desired effect on the windshield, allowing me to return home. There I welcomed myself with a hot water bottle on my back, a cup of hot mint tea, and a blanket pulled up under my chin.

Four days later the postal carrier brought me a package. I hadn't ordered anything. Still clad in my pajamas and heavy quilted bathrobe because of a slightly elevated temperature again, I examined the box. Scanning the brown paper wrapping for identifying information, I saw there was no return address. The handwriting was all wrong for my mother. Furthermore, the postmark was smeared but looked like Wellesley. I debated about opening it, fearing the worst, but finally acceded to my curiosity.

Inside, tenderly folded in white tissue paper was a delicate, ivory, vintage floor-length negligee and robe peignoir set of nylon trimmed in lace looking like part of a bridal trousseau. I was shocked. I threw the set back into the box and thought seriously about stomping on it. Instead, I re-wrapped it. Seething, I printed Benny's address in the left-hand corner, and marked the package, "Return to Sender."

When I went to the post office nearly a week later to send it back, Benny was there as well. "Good," I raised my hoarse voice, shoving the package into his hands. "I was about to send this back to you." Then I pulled him by his raincoat lapel to the side away from the line waiting for stamps. Trying not to cough again, I ticked off on my fingers my list of Don'ts for him to religiously follow: "Do not *send* or *give* me any more gifts. Do not *show up* where I am. Do not *call* me. You are *not* my protector. I do *not* want to see you ever again. If you continue to follow me or contact me in any way, I'll call the police. Is that crystal clear? No more. I mean it." His sad eyes crinkled as a small smile barely creased his cheeks. I muttered obscenities again under my breath, causing me to finally start coughing. Turning on heel, I strode to my car and didn't look back. I felt so impotent in this situation.

A month later a movie theater in West Newton was doing a Bogart Festival for two weeks, something like the one held at the Brattle Theater in Cambridge for the "Bogie Cult." I was more than ready to go, as was Alice from the farmers' market when I told her about it. Tonight was *The Caine Mutiny*. I loved that film because nobody rolled ball bearings like Bogie, tapping into genuine emotional complexity and what would then have been called "battle fatigue" in the basically insecure Captain Queeg.

Bogart was more than a cultural icon. He was a charismatic, consummate actor in creating his always-beautifully-nuanced roles. I promised myself I would likewise return when the theater played *Petrified Forest,* with his infamous portrayal of sociopathic gangster Duke Mantee; *Treasure of Sierra Madre* with his stark, greed-infused, maniacal Fred C. Dobbs; and *African Queen,* with his Academy Award Winning "Best Actor Oscar" role as the delightfully-eccentric Charlie Allnut. Before leaving for the six-thirty showing, I checked out the street. No one was parked or walking nearby. Leaving the lights on, I slipped out the front door and drove to the theater.

Surprisingly the theater was nearly empty. On the off-chance Benny was still following me, I had hoped it would be packed, providing me with anonymity and security in a mass of movie fans. With a large container of warm, buttery popcorn, I settled myself six rows from the screen. Shortly thereafter Alice joined me. Inveterate Bogart fans, we both were excited to see the film on the big screen again, having seen it as children and then many times on television. As we silently mouthed the dialogue along with the characters on the screen, we shared the wonderfully-fattening popcorn making it a hedonistic experience despite my usual vegetarian dietary and health consciousness.

Half-way through the film, when Fred MacMurray convinces Van Johnson to report Captain Queeg to Admiral Halsey on Halsey's flagship, I choked on a partially-popped kernel. Leaving my seat hurriedly so I wouldn't miss a second of MacMurray's deceptive, lying gutlessness, I sprinted up the aisle and out the door at the top to a water fountain in the lobby. Clearing my throat, I spotted a familiar figure. Hunching over, I scurried back to my aisle seat like a furtive beetle. There was no way I was going to let anyone chase me away from Bogie.

Crouched low in my seat, I tried to concentrate on the typhoon scene and popcorn. Alice and I whispered about the upcoming court martial procedure when Captain Queeg testifies and everything he says and does, especially about the missing quart of strawberries and his constant ball-bearing rolling, screams "paranoid personality disorder." We were discussing how Bogart deftly but subtly had Queeg butter his toast points with the compulsivity of a painter trying to create the perfect canvas when suddenly footsteps approached us. The deep-pile carpet crunched as long strides came nearer. Please let it be the usher, I fervently wished.

"Are you okay?" came the hushed words. "I saw you—."

"Shhhh! I cut him off, disgruntled.

Benny looked at Alice. "Move over," he commanded.

She looked at me, frowning, as if to say, "Who does this bozo think he is?" I rolled my eyes, sighed, and nodded that she should move before he created his own scene. I hadn't mentioned him to her or to anyone else. His behavior was hard to explain. But mostly I hadn't because I felt

Attracting and Dating the Wrong Men?

embarrassed I wasn't handling it well. Benny climbed over me and settled in.

José Ferrer, the defense counsel, was now at the hotel party for Van Johnson and Robert Francis's acquittal of mutiny charges, pointing out to Van Johnson and the other officers present that if they had supported the captain when he practically pleaded for their help, maybe Queeg wouldn't have broken during the typhoon ... and maybe there wouldn't have been any need for a mutiny. At the climax, Ferrer throws a glass of champagne in MacMurray's face, exposing to all assembled MacMurray's dastardly double dealing in general and lying at the court martial to "keep his own skirts from getting dirty." As soon as the credits finished, I rose from my seat but Benny took my arm. I shook him loose.

"Stop following me!"

"Following you?" He sounded incredulous. "I'm watching over you, *protecting* you." His voice rose as he looked at Alice with suspicion. "I'm trying to keep you safe. You're acting as if you don't appreciate what I do for you."

Alice glanced at me as if to ask if I needed help—maybe a well-placed karate chop or a weight-lifting usher. I shook my head "no." She mouthed, "If you need me, I'll be in the lobby for awhile," jerked her thumb in that direction, and moved diplomatically to the other side of the row in order to leave. The other patrons had already departed. Benny and I were standing alone in the theater. Gathering my coat around me and grabbing my handbag and popcorn pail, I pulled away from Benny, marched up the aisle, speaking over my shoulder, "I'm going home. Don't follow me again."

"You need me to keep you safe. There are lots of dangers out there."

"Leave me alone!" I trooped out, ignoring his pathetic, affected whimpering.

Before I knew it, it was almost Christmas. A large blanket of delicate six-sided radial crystals of frozen water covered the ground. Every thing looked pristine, clean, and enchanted. Fir boughs hung low under the precipitation's weight, creating cold-protective homes for small animals beneath them. Frozen, denuded branches reached into the partially-overcast sky like fragile glass spires. It felt like a world anew.

The holiday spirit was finally nudging its way into my mood. As I went about my business, I had for the most part erased Benny from my thoughts. I was no longer looking for his presence wherever I went. With his asphyxiating existence having retreated as a concern, I allowed myself to look forward to this Christmas.

Already in-hand was my plane ticket to see my mother in Florida for the holidays. My packing was nearly complete for this ten-day visit. My mother always did Christmas up right. She located large rug rolls, painted them white and then created spirals along their length with wide red satin ribbon to make them look like gigantic candy canes. Making extras, she donated them and hand-made wreaths to the Salvation Army, to perk up their various half-way houses, clothing stores, and donation sites for the holidays.

She had boxes of decorations we had made by hand when I was in the sixth grade and we couldn't afford to buy any. Somehow the glitter that had been glued to the papier-mâché apple- and orange shapes still shown brightly. The gold foil Polish stars, looking like rolled up gilt porcupines, were still unwrinkled and crisp, ever-ready to attach to the top of the tree or hang from balsam swags draped around her front door.

Everywhere she hung pomanders of oranges and apples decoratively pierced with cloves, allspice, and cinnamon sticks in red and green net bags with orris root and tied with gold ribbons. The spiced air reminded me of the aromatic

Scandinavian cookies she made for Christmas when I was a child. Like her mother, she made pepperkaker, with strong ginger; fattigmann, with cream and brandy; kringle, pretzel-like with cardamom and nutmeg; and krumkaker, shaped like embossed ice cream cones with lemon rind.

She had made red, fuzzy acrylic Santa hats with white pompoms and knitted red and green scarves for all her bears which she positioned around her apartment as if they were hairy Santa's elves. She had an impressive collection of unusual stuffed bears which kept her and her Himalayan cat, Lhotse, company. It never ceased to amaze me how beguiling everything looked and how satisfyingly fragrant everything smelled when she was finished with her decorating.

When the phone rang, I assumed it was Mother reminding me to bring some Norwegian goat cheese, specifically gjetost, and several cans of fish balls, a cod fish and potato flour product, from the nearby deli. Born in Norway but reared in New Jersey, she still loved all the Scandinavian delicacies her own mother cooked for them. Her mother used to make a monthly pilgrimage to a particular Brooklyn delicatessen for all the hard-to-find taste-bud memories. But to my disappointment it wasn't my mother.

"I want us to have Christmas together," he said.

"Benny, I told you not to call."

"I have a tree for us to decorate."

"We're not having Christmas together. I'm going out of town. Enjoy your holidays. Bye." I started to hang up.

"Wait," he called, "at least let me give you a tree. You have to have a tree. It's not Christmas without one. I have lights and decorations for it ... even if you don't want ... us ... to decorate it together. I'll bring them over to you in a half-hour. Well, actually, it might take me a little longer being on foot because of my crutches being hazardous on the ice."

Anxiety grabbed me by the throat. I bit my lip to keep from swearing at him then said, "Thanks but I don't want a tree. I want you to decorate it yourself and enjoy it."

Things had changed. Apparently he was no longer content to merely stalk and spy upon me to "protect" me. Now he wanted to take our "relationship" to a different level of interaction. Of course, the negligee he had sent had already signaled that. Grinding my molars together, I went back to finish an article about how a husband and wife financial business in Wellesley used personal communication in their marketing. It had a deadline of four o'clock for the *Townsman* which was rapidly approaching. I had no idea if Benny would actually attempt to hobble over but I wasn't willing to bet against it. I didn't want him at my house.

Because I would be away covering two weekly article submissions, I had those articles plus a third ready on the outside chance I was delayed. After typing the last few paragraphs, I threw on my Melton wool Navy pea coat that I'd purchased at the Army-Navy Store in Framingham, gathered the sheaf of papers, and drove directly to the newspaper office to drop them off on time. It was on One Crest Road, the hill next to the railroad station on Linden. After dropping off the articles and having a long conversation about the necessity of mentoring young people early in their careers with Beverly the editor, I headed back home.

As I pulled up onto Oakland Street, past Woodlawn Road, I saw Benny awkwardly limping along the side of the street with packages, heading in the direction of my house. Running him down crossed my mind, but, instead, I stopped beside him. Looking at me, he dropped his parcels and bent over on his wooden crutches looking pained, standing on one foot, holding a damp white foot-cast off the ground. Beside him was a potted, two-foot balsam fir, which looked heavy and awkward to carry, with a medium-size, handled paper bag bulging with tiny colored lights and decorations. He smiled, grimacing with discomfort, shifting his weight on his crutches. I alighted.

"You're probably wondering how I managed to get here with my injury. It was a struggle but I did it just for you. I did it because I wanted you to have a traditional family Christmas ... with us together."

"I told you 'no.'"

Sadly he shook his head. "You can't mean that. I thought when you saw the tree and the decorations you'd change your mind."

"No. No Christmas tree, no Christmas together."

"I don't understand how you can be so unappreciative of all I do for you. I show you how much I care and you treat me so cruelly. Well, if you won't allow us to decorate your tree together, can I at least come on over to your house to warm my frigid, wet, painful foot?" He winced for emphasis.

"No."

"You can't mean that. That's so uncharitable.

"Benny, the answer is still 'no.'"

"That's so cold and unfeeling. Will you at least do me the common courtesy of driving me back to my place so I don't have to hobble all the way back, further endangering the healing of my broken foot?"

I wanted to leave him standing there as I slipped into my car, started the engine, and slowly edged away from the edge of the uncurbed road. But I knew he'd keep walking to my house. Then what would I do if he banged on my door? If I'd have been more assertive, I would have let him bang on the door then called the police when he wouldn't leave. That sounded good, but—. I settled him in my car and drove him back to his place. I raged at myself for having been gulled again, having allowed him to manipulate me and my compassion. Moreover, I was sick of being angry with myself.

At his place I helped him keep his balance as he awkwardly, slowly ascended the three flights of stairs. As soon as he entered his apartment, he was on his way to his small kitchen. I could hear the clatter of his kettle against the old porcelain sink and the rush of water. Apparently he was putting on water for coffee or tea as I headed back down to hoist his holiday load from the car.

After re-ascending the stairs and dropping off the tree and decorations inside his front door, I took a minute to glance around his living room. Even in the daylight it looked dreary. The walls were painted an apple-green so popular in the 1950s. The three windows were covered by yellowing pull-down shades and faded floral half-curtains. His only decorations were two unframed, faded movie posters of low-budget horror films from the fifties. One was the 1954 *Creature from the Black Lagoon.* It pictured a huge dark-green prehistoric beast holding a struggling, screaming, scantily-clad, long-legged female, so typical of 1950's pulp fiction covers. The other was the 1956 *The She-Creature.* It showed a huge, dark-reddish prehistoric creature standing behind another barely draped, bosom-y and leggy female who was going to be hypnotically regressed to become the creature. Each was attached to a wall with peeling masking tape.

It flashed to me that he really ought to have the poster of Don Siegel's 1956 classic, *Invasion of the Body Snatchers.* Made from Jack Finney's 1955 science-fiction/horror book of the same name, it was on the surface about panspermia theory which suggests that seeds from space could float to Earth and take root, ultimately taking over. But written during the time of Senator Joseph McCarthy's Red Scare and the House Un-American Committee Hearings about Communists, it was also a parable about the ideology and politics of that time. Specifically, it demonstrated how McCarthyism was malevolently insinuating itself into people's lives, like an alien being taking over their thoughts and emotions and controlling them, creating an environment of hysteria and a social witch hunt. The poster for the film was dramatically simple, capturing the rampant fear. It had stars Kevin McCarthy and Dana Wynter small, on a yellow background, running from a huge black hand-print against a red background. It was one of those entertaining movies that gave you lots to think about on different levels.

With my mind having switched back to leaving, I took the door handle in my right hand and called, "I'm leaving. Enjoy your holiday. Good-bye." But before I could slip out the door, Benny had already emerged from the kitchen with two mugs of some steaming dark, tea-like substance, balanced above his crutches. He put them down on the coffee table. Hopping toward me, he grabbed my left hand tightly. His palm was warm and moist.

"You can't go yet. If we can't decorate our tree together, at least we can have some holiday hot spiced tea together." With that he tried to pull me along to the faded floral sofa behind the coffee table. I balked and yanked my left hand from his clutch. In doing so, however, I lost my balance. I fell forward and tangled with one of his crutches. Twisting, I landed backwards, just barely on the cushions.

Likewise losing his tenuous balance as his left crutch slid forward, he toppled, landing on top of me nearly face to face, pinning me to the sofa. "No! Stop!" I shouted with every ounce of angry strength I possessed. In an instant I shifted position. My feet gained purchased with the floor and my free arm slid under me to lever me up, thrusting and rolling my upper body forward. He stumbled backward onto his right foot which gave out under him, landing him ingloriously in a sitting position on the floor. His back slapped against the walnut coffee table which he shoved a foot farther into the living room, spilling the tea.

"I want you out of my life ... now!" I rose from the sofa and turned to go.

"But we are meant to be together. I know down deep you know it too. I knew it from the moment I first saw you. It's destiny."

"No, Benny, it's not destiny! I'm going. I want you out of my life."

"But I'm even divorcing my wife to be with you."

I nearly choked. His wife? Was this more game-playing?

Struggling to right himself and get his crutches securely under his arms, he slipped on the ragged, multi-colored, braided area rug under the coffee table and sprawled on the floor facedown.

I considered leaving him there, figuring he'd right himself eventually. After all, the problem was his foot not his knees, hips, or back. On second thought, I reached down to give him a hand. Hoping I could finally get him to hear me and end this once and for all, I decided to take a different tack with him.

"I'm sure you're a great guy but I do *not* have feelings for you. If I've inadvertently ever said or done *anything* that led you to think that we would ever have a relationship—be together, I apologize. It has never been what I wanted. It's not what I want now."

He looked at me, pathos, defeat, and confusion emanating from his face and body like waves of electromagnetic energy. He seemed unable to comprehend I didn't acknowledge "our pre-ordained romance." As I helped him sit on the sofa then stood in front of him, his face began to change almost imperceptibly. I could practically see the thoughts twisting and turning in his mind, his emotions and questions creating shadows on his face. He had had a similar look in the theater in West Newton when he came upon Alice and me.

His head bowed, slowing shaking back and forth, he said, "I don't understand. I have bent over backwards for you to be the perfect gentleman. I have kept my hands to myself because I respected you. I have watched over you, protected you, and kept you safe. I have always been there for you for over nine months. I have showered you with gifts, my attention, and my caring. I have acceded to all your many demands without complaint. And now you're rejecting me? After all I've done for you?"

Although I had my back to the front door, ready to leave, I thought perhaps I had better wait until he finished. His agitation was growing stronger. I was concerned that he might retaliate if I didn't hear him out. Showcasing his thoughts on his face, Benny's furrowed brow suggested the pieces were coalescing, making their way from his brain to his lips. Suddenly he opened his eyes wide as if a conclusion had come to him.

"It's not about me. It's never been about me," he said with a wave of relief. "It's so much simpler. I couldn't put my finger on it until now. Finally it all makes sense. You're always in the farmers' market talking with Alice. I've seen you two running together. In the theater you two were sitting huddled together, giggling, sharing popcorn!" He paused then barked at me, "You don't love me because you love her! You're a lesbian!" It was as if he had driven the last spike into the last tie of the rail line linking the Central Pacific and Union Pacific at Promontory Point, Utah. He had his aha.

He had reconfigured everything to relieve himself of responsibility for my not caring for him. He had found a way to save face. I watched his features darken with anger and repugnance and his upper lip curl. He shouted at me, "After all the love and attention I've wasted on you! And now this betrayal! Get out of my house! Never come back!"

I grabbed and twisted the door knob. Once in the hall, I quickly descended the three flights of stairs. I couldn't wait to get away from him. I flung open the squeaking front door and strode to my car, slipping on the icy walkway. It threw me to my knees but I didn't feel the pain. My thoughts were tumbling helter-skelter as I turned over the ignition and sped home. Could it really be over? I asked myself.

As a result of my finally having pricked his romantic-fantasy balloon and left his ego on life support, I worried that in his delusion he would see me now as someone who had led him on. The question in my mind was would he come after me seeking revenge? Moreover, what could I do if he did?

At one point I had made a hollow threat to call the police. But what could the police have done in reality? The law at that time was not on my side. Unless he had physically threatened me, harmed me, broken into my home, or destroyed my property, there was nothing they could do. He was simply an amorous suitor and I should be the one to find a way to handle him.

Much to my relief I did not see or hear from him again. Apparently his so-called revelation about me had both embarrassed and discouraged him. I discovered he moved soon thereafter. When it was all over, I realized that I had been extremely lucky that he hadn't retaliated. As I later learned, stalkers often do.

* *

Resulting Awareness: Even feeling and acting more assertively, I discovered that when unusual situations cropped up, I was less primed to be immediately assertive. It was a matter of belief, confidence, and practice. Slowly I was giving myself permission to not be held back by early allegiances, forbiddances, and gender-role expectations.

The question I asked myself: What could I have done to have handled this situation better and what could I do differently in the future?

* * *

9

MARCELLO

When I was working at Massachusetts Institute of Technology in Cambridge, I was ensconced in the Mechanical Engineering Department as an information specialist. The project on which I was working was to create a computerized textile thesaurus for the U.S. Bureau of Standards under the auspices of the Department of Commerce. Most of those with whom I worked were graduate students. Occasionally a researcher from outside would come in to see what we were doing with systematizing our data.

One time it was a small, thin Chinese engineer who was a few months pregnant. This poor soul was constantly, desperately ill with morning sickness. Everyday she seemed even thinner and paler than the day before. I had never previously seen anyone in such dire straits while attempting to put in a full day's work. Often I worried I would have to call for EMTs or get her medical assistance at MIT's health clinic. Somehow she hung in, doing her job.

After several months, however, she disappeared, apparently having been corralled by a seemingly insensitive husband. I couldn't imagine puking my guts out before and during work while the person I expected to be supportive of me constantly spoke critically to me, displaying no empathy whatsoever. Too many times I was tempted to intrude where I wasn't wanted, and certainly not invited, to say something.

How he acted under non-pregnancy circumstances I had no idea. I hoped it was only the strain of her condition that had set him off. But for him to treat her so badly in public convinced me he no longer deserved the benefit of my doubt. Whether that was his culture's patriarchy showing itself or his own meanness, I didn't care. How she made out afterward with her pregnancy, engineering career, and husband I never heard.

Following her was a part-time researcher from Washington, D.C., who was working with the International Atomic Energy Agency (IAEA) on generalized systematized information databases. He was Dr. Marcello Primatore. Thirty-four years to my twenty-eight, he was five-seven, slim, with dark-chocolate-brown hair and a receding hairline. However, he had the most mesmerizing cinnamon-flecked eyes, kissed by long lashes, and the most delightful, soul-enveloping smile I had ever seen. His whole face seemed to glow incandescently when he smiled. While I didn't believe in "love at first sight," I did believe in the "force of attraction between an electron and a proton."

Initially we were together only intermittently during work, exchanging brief pleasantries when we met in passing in the hall or in the computer lab. I tended to spend all my time tied up in either inputting textile information or checking reams of printouts in my office. Several weeks of increasing nods, smiles, and brief conversations went by quickly. It was frustrating because I detected some interest and wanted to explore it. However, he always seemed to be tied up with others on the project or hopping planes back to D.C.

What we needed was an opportunity to be together for longer periods of time. It occurred to me that we both could make use of the long, wide table in the department library to spread out, collate, check data, and talk. The next time I passed him in the hall I gave him my best smile and handed him a note telling him about the table's accessibility. To my delight the following afternoon he appeared, smiling, and availed himself of one end of the ample surface while I used the other.

From that day on he appeared with some frequency when I was there. I made a point of doing my work there instead of in my office whenever I could. Consequently, both of us spent a little less time assiduously checking data than talking. It was then I began noticing something peculiar. As romance-novel-clichéd as it sounded to me, every time I looked into his eyes, I experienced a sense of losing my balance and falling into what they would have referred to as his "deep pools of limpid waters." This was the sort of emotion I had earlier pooh-poohed as a fiction resulting from the genre writer's overheated gonads. Yet it was disconcertingly real in a magnetically enticing way.

"Tell me about yourself," I suggested as soon as he joined me and had settled himself into a chair near me.

Smiling warmly, he said, "I teach theoretical and applied mechanics at the University of Maryland. That's what I received my doctorate in from the University of Illinois."

"Maybe you can share some of your publications with me. I'd like to know more about what you've done. So, I take it you've lived in the U.S. for awhile now."

"About fifteen years. I received both my master's and doctorate in theoretical and applied mechanics then began teaching."

"Do I assume correctly you were born in Italy?"

"No, in fact, I wasn't. I was born in Tripoli."

"Really. That's very interesting. I want to hear more about that when we have more time. How much longer will you be working here in Cambridge on your project?"

"I expect to finish my research here within the month. I've been coming here intermittently for a few years. I'll be heading back to D.C. and after that, I've been asked to head an international committee for the IAEA in Milan."

My heart dropped. "That sounds exciting and very prestigious ... and I'm sure it is well-deserved," I offered, trying to add some enthusiasm to my voice where I felt none. I didn't really know anything about him as a person yet and wanted more time in which to find it out. In the meantime I discovered I was getting bogged down in more of those embarrassingly soppy thoughts, like "I felt I'd always known him." After another week of small conversations, sharing anecdotes, jokes, experiences, and observations on the fly or over printouts, he asked me out to dinner. I was elated. So one late afternoon at the end of a hot, humid August day we would be getting to know each other better.

MIT's Mechanical Engineering Department resided on the second floor of the School of Architecture and Planning building, located at 37 Massachusetts Avenue. Walking through the large first-floor rotunda, we approached the glass entryway. Beyond its numerous fluted, round concrete columns was a waterfall of eighteen broad, concrete steps spilling down in a rush to the sidewalk below. As we descended, I could see boxwoods, firs, pines, and flowering shrubs on either side of the entry way, luxuriantly hugging the foundation of this long concrete building. Pin oaks, maple and elm trees lined the wide sidewalks and were fully leafed providing a shady path.

Strolling westward along Massachusetts Avenue on our way to Harvard Square, we passed older brick apartment buildings on our right which sported small patches of carefully manicured grass surrounding a profusion of blossoming azaleas in magenta, red, pinks, white, or yellow. These residences were interspersed with miniscule asphalt parking lots for their renters. The farther we walked, the fewer residences there were. They had been replaced by squat, cement-constructed, mini-malls which appeared to hug the ground in case of intra-plate earthquakes which occasionally struck areas along the New England coast.

In a few minutes we passed Old Cambridge Baptist Church on Harvard Street to our right. Built of field stone and granite in American Gothic Revival architecture, it was striking. Made up of massing asymmetrical forms, it boasted arching, graceful, delicate Gothic stained glass windows with Tiffany window bridges. It also had the red church door to, perhaps, mark it as a sanctuary or keep pursuers or the Devil at bay.

The office of the *Harvard Crimson*, the Nation's oldest continuously published daily college newspaper, which was founded in 1873 and incorporated in 1967, was just down Plympton. About a block from Massachusetts Avenue on the left, it was situated in a Georgian brick building. Its former-editors included Presidents Franklin D. Roosevelt and John F. Kennedy, Pulitzer-Prize-winning journalist and historian, David Halberstam, and novelist Michael Crichton. Cambridge, like Boston, was an historical joy to behold on foot.

At the Square students from MIT, Radcliffe, and Harvard were in crowds everywhere in front of the Harvard Coop, aka the Harvard-MIT Cooperative Store, on Brattle Street. The overflow occupied the MBTA, the Massachusetts Bay Transit Authority, stop a short distance away. Standing around, riding by or resting on bicycles, and walking with backpacks, they were a mass of youthful enthusiasm and optimism. Besides enjoying the last days of summer's freedom, they were likely gearing up for a new semester or quarter, depending upon which school they attended.

As we swung to the right on Massachusetts Avenue, there was an East Indian restaurant just a few steps away. I had never had East Indian food but Marcello, who had traveled more extensively than I and was a connoisseur of international fare, had. Letting him take the lead since he knew about the individual dishes, I noticed our Indian waiter seemed to heartily approve of Marcello ordering. His attitude held no meaning for me until after we placed our order. I noticed that same waiter grimaced when a female seated with several males ordered for herself. He kept trying to have a man order for her. Obviously he thought this was inappropriate behavior on her part. I suspected he wondered why these men weren't doing what he expected them to do—take the lead, make the decision.

Ironically, years later, I experienced this myself when I was in London. In an East Indian restaurant the East Indian waiter did not want to take my order. He kept rebuffing me, prompting my male companion to place it for me, which, to his credit, he would not do. My thought at the time was, "You're in a cosmopolitan city and your native cultural rules don't apply when serving the general public. So deal with it."

While that waiter finally took my order to prevent us from leaving as we had threatened to do, he continued to make jibes at my companion's "masculinity" for not controlling "his" woman and putting her in her "proper place." Upon paying the bill, we let the manager, also ostensibly East Indian, know there was a problem with this waiter's disrespectful and off-putting attitude and behavior. Since he made some excuse for him, I wondered if he would pass on the complaint to his employee.

Marcello suggested we start with mulligatawny, a traditional lentil soup with herbs and spices; followed by bhajia, vegetable fritters; tandoori chicken, a sort of barbecue; and finished with gulab jamun, an evaporated milk dumpling dipped in rose syrup served warm and topped with crushed pistachios. Even though I had required him to eat most of my portions, I was overly satiated. I had never eaten that much at one meal before. But since it had been such a fascinating gustatory journey through India, I had put forth some belly-expanding effort.

Attracting and Dating the Wrong Men?

As we chatted throughout the meal, my travel guide had been looking at me with soft eyes in the flickering candle light. That sweet smile and those eyes held me fast. I could see myself in them, feeling my breathless anticipation and our mutual desire. Upon leaving the restaurant and in need of exercise after such a goodly repast, we sauntered into Harvard Yard. This is twenty-five tree-filled, grassy acres of crisscrossing paths, adjacent to the Square. After walking awhile, we found a wrought iron bench under the downy leaf cover where we spent hours discussing everything, sharing, and staring into each other's eyes.

"While I am Italian," he said, "I was born in Libya and spent my childhood in North Africa, Italy, and South Africa, specifically in Cape Town. My father was in wine-making there."

We talked about winemaking then I briefly contributed my having lived in many different places around the U.S. because my father had been in sales in my earlier life. Fleshing out his history that he had only touched upon briefly before, he said, "I received my Bachelor's Degree in Civil Engineering. I got my Diploma at the University of London before I came here, to the U.S."

I shared my less exhaustive education to date, which had not as yet included my doctorate in medicine or in anything else, and my broad, less exotic, though sometimes eccentric, travels around the U.S. He seemed sincerely interested in some of my out-of-the-ordinary adventures. His interest was captivating and encouraging. I wondered sadly if I would ever feel this comfortable with and appreciated by any other man.

As it approached ten o'clock, with the moon rising, buoyed up on the heat of our passions, he invited me back to his apartment. I was sorely tempted. My tissues were engorged and well-lubricated and my body was shouting, "Yes!" But as seductive as his invitation was, I reluctantly said, "No."

Rosa, a second-generation Italian friend, had warned me at length about *real* Italian men. Twenty-four years my senior, she traveled to Italy frequently and indicated she knew the real scoop on them, "They'll do anything—even be amazingly sweet, tender, and attentive—to get you into bed, and then it's 'ciao, baby' Believe me, you'll be just another notch in his *maschilismo*. It doesn't matter what he does for a living. They all have strong standards of masculinity to uphold."

In several weeks Marcello was to leave for Washington. I felt bad. I had just gotten to know him better after all that time we worked in the same department. Now we were talking and laughing together whenever we could snatch a few precious minutes. The attraction was so strong for me. But there was so little time available in which to evaluate if there were really anything between us that could possibly be developed. In reality it was ridiculous to think about the potential of our ever having any kind of "relationship." He would be in D.C. before going to Italy and I would be here. Still ... daydreams and desires die hard.

After more short chats and coffees together, the time had arrived for him to fly away. The evening before he was to leave, we hiked around Cambridge. Along Massachusetts Avenue to Western Avenue, then west toward Memorial Drive, we traveled southward until we found a wooden bench overlooking the river. Arching branches with deep green and chartreuse leaves swayed and whispered cooling sounds in the slightest feather-stirring breeze. Before us was the Charles with the luminescence of Boston across the water. Delicately dancing scintillations on its black velvet surface darted like faeries as the sunlight vanished, painting a soft-hued sky. He absorbed me with his eyes, his smile, his tenderness, and his attentiveness. It felt something like an out-of-body experience. I didn't care what generalizations Rosa made about Italian men and their romantic sorcery techniques. Whether or not it was true about Marcello, I felt deeply and irretrievably besotted ... and I was about to lose my "dearest, most beloved friend."

We were half-way back to my car parked on Vassar Street, on the other side of the School of Architecture and Planning building, when it began to pour in dollops. Without any raingear, umbrella, or even a newspaper to protect us, we both were getting soaked as we ran, rain dripping off our noses. My hair which I wore up at work was plastered to my head. My tan linen suit clung to me like a second skin and my feet were squishing in my beige low-heeled shoes. His lightweight brown flannel coat and Italian shoes were quickly polka-dotted with large spreading blots of wetness. I wondered how he would salvage them, if indeed he could.

When we reached my car, he reached into his inside jacket pocket and handed me a still-dry package. Opening it as carefully as I could to try to prevent its getting wet, I saw it was a paperback of E.M. Forster's *A Room with a View.* It's the story of a young woman traveling in Florence, Italy, seeking freedom from the sexual repression of her time, growing up, and finding true love. It was Forster's most romantic and optimistic book. Marcello had inscribed it, "With it goes a little bit of me." I felt my heart open up. I wanted to grab him and hold him tight to my bosom forever.

We kissed. It was a three-day kiss, full of bottomless passion, longing, and infinite possibilities ... at least on my part. Then we said what felt like the most gut-wrenching good-bye I had yet to experience, except for the death of a loved one. As I slipped into my car, he stood behind it, looking at me through the back window. Water was gushing down the street gutter splashing on his pant legs where he stood, covering his shoes. He raised his hand to wave as I pulled out. In my rearview mirror I could see him, still in the street, his hand lingering, moving back and forth, in the air, making no effort to get out of the rain or the street's flood. I started to cry to the rhythmic swishing of the windshield wipers as they tried mechanically to clear my path home.

When I told Rosa how he had watched me until I disappeared, getting drenched, she dismissed it as more of the same, "It was all an act." She continued, "I told you. That's what Italian men do. They'll do *anything* to make that charming, romantic 'you're the one and only love of my life for eternity … and longer' impression."

"You can't be serious. You think that he'd risk ruining his flannel jacket and shoes to fulfill some traditional convention, to make the 'grand gesture' for someone he would never see again. I can't believe that. Besides, he's an engineer."

"He's an *Italian* engineer. Italian men ooze with charm and loving attention despite any obstacles, at any cost. In fact, the more obstacles and the more challenges, the better. They can woo and make *any* woman—young or old, fat or thin, ugly or beautiful—feel beautiful." He had certainly done that. "They can make you feel open to anything they suggest …*anything*." He had done that too. "I really wouldn't make too much of it or think too much about it if I were you."

Getting thoroughly soaked to demonstrate some cultural approach to romanticism seemed to me to be a bit of a stretch. I wanted to talk myself into her being wrong about him, that he was different. I had no idea if such strong cultural expectations would extend to ruining his wardrobe as a "gesture." But philosophical questions didn't really matter because he was leaving for D.C. in the morning.

I never expected to feel this way again about anyone—and, sadly, I *never* did—so I clung tightly to this memory and the wish that his behavior had been because he cared for me as a person in some way, and not as some object of obligatory sexual actions. I wanted Rosa to be exaggerating, mistaken, envious, or attempting to convince me of her deep knowledge of and experience with Italian men and their techniques.

Attracting and Dating the Wrong Men?

In October we had completed the computer-printout thesaurus: *Thesaurus of Textile Terms Covering Fibrous Materials and Processes*. It contained 8,000 key terms and 72,000 relationships. Its coverage was designed to serve the needs of fiber producers, textile manufacturers, clothing distributors, manufacturers of textile auxiliaries and dyes, manufacturers of textile machinery, governmental laboratories for materials testing, as well as retailing and consumer organizations. Soon to become an incomparable reference work in the field, it was published by the MIT Press in Cambridge then shipped off to the Bureau of Standards. The 448-page book even had my name gracing the title page along those of with Drs. Backer and Valko as its editors.

With that finished, my mother and I decided to pull up stakes and move to Southern California with the intention of making a fresh start. Our route would take us through D.C. So on the off-chance Marcello might welcome another encounter, I let him know. To my very pleasant surprise, even though we had to-date exchanged infrequent letters, he enthusiastically agreed. Reaching our destination early, Mother and I made quick stops at the Lincoln Memorial, Washington Monument on the national mall, and the six-hundred-acre grounds of Arlington National Cemetery. We arrived just in time to see the changing of the guard by members of the U.S. Third Infantry Regiment which maintained the 'round-the-clock vigil of the Tombs of the Unknowns. The "Old Guard" was the oldest active-duty Army infantry unit, having served since 1784. If only we had had much more time, we would have hit the U.S. Botanic Garden as well. Established in 1820, it is a living plant museum and one of the oldest botanic gardens in North America. When I let Marcello know we had arrived, he picked me up at our motel to take me to his apartment.

While it was unmistakable that he wanted intimacy, he was more sweetly eager than obnoxious about it for which I would be forever grateful there were no attempts at a wrestling match. Since I knew we'd never see each other again, I felt I couldn't let myself follow my desires as much as I wanted to. Rosa's words still echoed in the deepest vaults of my mind. I didn't want to think of myself as a "one-night-stand," that notch in his belt he had yet to achieve.

Irrespective of whether I would have ecstatically enjoyed myself or not, I didn't want to feel I had done it because it was "expected" of me by a male. I wasn't emotionally ready to give myself permission to enjoy myself for myself irrespective of the circumstance. Instead, we talked about everything, gazed longingly into each other's eyes, and petted deliriously until it was five in the morning—when he drove me back to my motel. In spite of his apparent sexual frustration, he was nothing but a gentleman about it. Was that how Italian men were "supposed" to act? Maybe he was simultaneously both proving and disproving Rosa's calculus.

I have thought of him often and the way he made me feel. It was so unlike the way any of the American men I had met or dated made me feel. With him I felt so valued, accepted, respected, gently attended to, so special, as one with unplumbed depths and potential. He had made me love him ... and love myself as well. When he had taken his post in Milan, I received another letter from him. I replied but knew that was very probably the last of our correspondence.

Four decades later I tracked him down through Google and found that his international career had continued to be illustrious. After leaving his research at MIT, he worked his way up to being head of a section at the International Nuclear Information System. Finding him revived all my submerged feelings of unrequited lost love. He was now retired, residing part-time in Italy and part-time in Austria.

Recently I had even considered writing to him ... but to what end? Irrespective of whatever the reality might have been, I preferred to continue to believe he had truly cared all those years ago ... and I still have his book. When I remember our fleeting moments together, I think of Carole King's lyrics in "Love for the Last Time" from the movie *Murphy's Romance*: "He kissed me like a lover and loved me like a friend." Even though that song is finished, the melody lingers on.

* *

Resulting Awareness: Because of the attraction I experienced, I tended to regress a little to gender-role expectations about how I should act. I was worried about being negatively evaluated and rejected so I was slower and less assertive in letting him know I wanted to get to know him better. Having acted on my desires earlier would potentially have given us more time to evaluate our relationship. However, I did make the right choice about not having sex at that time so I felt good about being assertive in that respect.

The question I asked myself: How could I use that feeling of unconditional acceptance I took from my perception of our relationship and successfully build upon it?

* * *

Signe A. Dayhoff, PhD

Heeding the call for letter writers, I wrote to our troops in Vietnam for about eights months. The USO, United Service Organizations, a non-profit providing programs, services, and entertainment to the troops, had been looking for people to write to soldiers, sailors, airmen, and marines. To become a correspondent, I sent a brief, snappy-peppy biography and a Polaroid of myself sitting on my navy blue Scandinavian sofa wearing a rose-colored wraparound with my long hair waved on top of my head. The next thing I knew I was being inundated with letters from military men who wanted to write. Thirty service personnel had chosen me to help keep them sane in the worst, most distressing circumstances they could imagine. While their reaching out to me was daunting, it felt good to be accepted and be of help.

Under a constant shroud of fear and the icy clutch of hopeless and despairing dread, they demonstrated how glad they were to have a link with home and with a "pretty girl." I was someone to whom they could send sketches they had done, cartoons cut from the military paper, photos of themselves, poems and short stories they had composed, and pour out their hearts, unfettered by shyness, in long letters. Not knowing how their mail delivery would be, I reciprocated twice a week to each individual. I did know a cheery letter could possibly make a positive difference in how they felt and approached their frightening tasks. Unfortunately, I had no idea how that heightened positive emotion might be construed with respect to me.

* * *

10

TULLY

One young man named Tully from Mississippi spent most of his days—day after day after day—in the hot humid sun or heavy rain, keeping his head down under enemy fire, in soaking boots, fighting foot fungus, snakes, and stinging insects. As a result, he was extraordinarily delighted to have my letters in his life. However, my nice, newsy letters took on an inordinately emotional significance for him. Unbeknownst to me, he quickly had put me on a pedestal. In fact, it wasn't long before his letters showed hints that he felt I was the *one and only one* who could ultimately make his life perfect and complete when he got out of the service. That was a frightening and unexpected result.

Because I understood how stress could distort and amplify a person's feelings of attraction to others, I was very careful in all my letters to everyone to be pleasant, funny, as interesting as possible, but impersonal. However, to individuals trying merely to survive in such a traumatic environment, anyone who showed any interest or kindness could easily be misinterpreted to mean so much more. My being aware of that, however, didn't help me deal with Tully's rapidly-increasing feelings for me.

Consequently, it wasn't long before the expected happened. Despite my attempts to get us back on track, he wanted me to visit him and meet his family when he returned to the States. If he not been in such a life-threatening situation when he received my letters, he very likely would not have felt that way about me, much less with that intensity. Of course, if he had not been in such a dangerous happenstance, he and I would never have "met" and corresponded in the first place.

When he said he wanted me to visit, I thanked him but refused his offer. He questioned why not. He was going to pay my way. Refusing to accept my negative responses, he kept on expressing his need for me to visit. Because I didn't feel I should have to have an "excuse," that my saying "no" was sufficient, it had not occurred to me that making up a story to give me a reason I *couldn't* accede to his wishes might be useful. Consequently, even though I had given him a definite "no," a letter arrived with a round-trip ticket stating, "You have to come!"

We talked on the phone. I said, "No." He said, "Yes." He was adamant. "It's the least I can do for all you've done for me while I was up to my ass in mud and snakes, dodging bullets, fighting the Cong day and night, and hoping not to be fragged or napalmed." I wanted to just send it back but my father's expectations of what I "should" do came to mind. I finally agreed, but most regretfully. Once again I was unassertively doing something I didn't want to do, but was expected to do. It was against my better judgment. Once I finally agreed, he told me, "Bring a hat and gloves with you."

"A hat and gloves" struck me as a strange requirement. The only thing that occurred to me was there was going to be some kind of special ceremony being given by his home town for returning veterans that he thought required more formality. I never wore hats, except, of course, to keep my head warm in winter. I wore gloves only when playing pool. Then they were short black leather gloves that helped suggest that I *really* played the game. His command required me to scrounge up something chapeau-like. I did find an acrylic-fiber beret in off-white I could wear with a red-and-off-white polyester-blend dress I could take. The white cotton dress gloves I borrowed from an old trunk belonging to my mother where she had packed them away in moth balls, a nostalgic reminder of her 1950s' life.

Meeting me at the airport on Saturday morning, Tully surprised me, and not a little. He bore little resemblance to his photo taken in Southeast Asia that he had initially sent. He had gained over fifty pounds. Now he reminded me of a large chipmunk with full cheek pouches and little piggy eyes trying to peer over them. What became apparent in-person that hadn't been apparent in his letters was that he was a "good ol' country boy" in his mannerisms, behavior, and cultural expectations—all of which was foreign to me. Having come from the Northeast, I was anything but, and out of my element.

Despite our nearly three-months'-long correspondence, I immediately realized I knew nothing about him as a person, other than that he had two brothers and had had a puppy at one time. His letters had been about his daily war experiences, his working to retain his sanity, and staying alive. Unfortunately he seemed to believe he "knew" all he needed to know about me from what he had created and solidified in his fear-enhanced romantic fantasy.

Because he was overjoyed to see me, he repeatedly hugged me, unwilling to stop praising my virtues when I arrived at his family's home. I was at a singular disadvantage, rapidly becoming embarrassed at having to continually dismiss his accolades because of their extreme exaggeration. His mother seemed very pleasant and welcoming. But, at the same time, she seemed concerned that her son had poured all his hopes and dreams into me. Furthermore, he was moving far too fast, way too soon after returning from tumult of fighting a war.

In reality, no matter how careful I tried to be in my letters, I had little control over how he or anyone else interpreted my words and intentions. I had never told any of my thirty correspondents that there were twenty-nine others. After all, they had chosen me; I hadn't chosen them. Hopefully they realized others might have contacted me as well. It seemed unnecessarily cruel to make a point that they were not the only one to whom I was writing, that they were merely "another stamp on another envelope," another faceless fighting force in a Vietnam war newsreel. Their feeling acknowledged as individuals would allow them to feel comfortable sharing their lives when they most needed to.

Tully's behavior toward me was way over the top for my being simply a conscientious letter writer. Returning his round-trip ticket to him with or without some earth-shaking excuse would have been a lot less painful for him than my having to back out of his future-life expectations in person. And as a result of my unassertiveness, I was in quicksand up to my hip bones and sinking fast in a no-win situation.

His mother had set me up is a tiny room next to the bathroom which was long and narrow with a door lock that didn't always latch properly. Without success I searched for something to use as a door stop. As a result, I constantly worried someone, one of his two brothers or Tully, would barge right on in when I was using the toilet or taking a shower. However, despite my fears, there were no accidental entries during my weekend stay.

The toilet seat was another problem. His brothers had painted it black. In the inordinate humidity it was still sticky to the touch. What they used, oil-based house paint or spray-on acrylic, was a question. But irrespective, my not wishing to touch the toilet seat with any part of my body or clothing meant having to acrobatically balance or learn to levitate in order to relieve myself.

Attracting and Dating the Wrong Men?

Tully was so glad to be home that all he wanted to was drive around and visit all his old friends with me in tow. After a pleasant early-evening Saturday Southern dinner, including grits and okra, prepared by his mother and eaten with his family, we hopped into his car to make the rounds. I didn't know what to expect. When we had driven only a short distance in the increasing dark, he suddenly stopped at a distance from what looked like a food establishment in the middle of nowhere. Oddly we parked quite short of its parking lot where there was no lighting. Upon my more careful inspection, the storefront looked like an ice cream parlor. I wondered if this were the first visitation on his scheduled circuit, seeing an old pal who worked there. But why were we parking so far away ... where it was so dark? Without a word, he opened the driver's door, alighted, and walked down the gravel driveway, crossed the illuminated parking lot, and disappeared inside. Minutes passed. I sat there mulling over what I should do. Was I supposed to get out and join him and his friend? That felt presumptuous. If he had wanted me to come along, he would have said so, wouldn't he? As a result, I continued to wait and wait and wait ... by myself ... in the dark.

After more than ten minutes, I was getting antsy. Finally he reappeared with something large in his hand. I couldn't tell what it was. But as he came closer, I could see it was a foot-long, boat-like ice cream sundae-to-go. Was that ice cream intended for the two of us? I hoped he wasn't expecting us to share it. That was too intimate, I squirmed. But as it turned out, I need not have worried.

After wordlessly and carefully resettling himself behind the wheel, he commenced eating it ... all by himself. Totally focused, he seemed enraptured by it. I kept waiting for him to moan aloud with orgasmic pleasure with every bite. To be certain to capture every last molecule to savor on his tongue, he scraped the receptacle of it coating and licked the spoon.

When he was through, he threw the plastic ice cream dish into the trash container near the car, started the engine, and resumed his journey.

Quizzically wrinkling my brow, I asked myself what had just happened. It seemed pretty clear. *He* had wanted some dessert so he had gotten *himself* some dessert. End of story. I felt like Dorothy speaking to her dog, "We're not in Kansas anymore, Toto."

Next we drove to a small bar in someone's basement. I couldn't tell if it were a commercial establishment as well. It seemed to be set up that way. Here he introduced me to all those present, "This is the girl who wrote to me in 'Nam" with a quick side-shoulder hug and a smile. Once that was out of the way, he became involved in their discussions, leaving me abandoned, seated by myself on a stool at the bar with no one to talk to. I was some ten feet away from where twelve of them, seated and standing, were gathered around a table. Forty-five minutes later, having shared stories with each of them and been brought up to date on all their lives, the community, and gossip, he made his farewell. From there we left to hit several other places, including a friend's house and a card game, each with similar results.

Sunday morning Tully "instructed" me to put on my dress, hat, and gloves. His directions reminded me of an incident that occurred when the manager of a luncheon shop at Shoppers World in Framingham, Howard, did the same thing when he asked me to dinner. For about a week he had flirted outrageously with me when I came in for lunch. I was working in Jordan Marsh department store while taking classes at night. When I said "yes," he gave me strict instructions about how I should dress: I should look semi-seductive yet very business-like. While I liked to know the particular ambiance of a restaurant or the purpose of my being at some occasion so I could dress accordingly, I did not like being told what to wear or how to wear it. I could and would accommodate any situation apparel-wise with appropriateness and style, thank you very much.

When Howard picked me up that evening, he seemed very pleased we were going out and with how I looked. It felt like a compliment. At the restaurant just as our appetizers arrived, we were joined, unannounced, by a middle-aged man in a dark business suit. After Howard introduced me to him, they began to talk about some entrepreneurial venture they had been previously discussing. They talked through the entrée and dessert. I remained silent, nodding knowingly and smiling at appropriate times to reinforce their agreements, as if scripted. The possibility of this having been a random happening was quickly extinguished. I was not amused.

On the way home I asked Howard what that had been all about. He explained, "I was trying to close a big deal with this man and wanted to make a good final impression. I thought you would do that." He hadn't asked my out because he really wanted to date me.

Appalled, I indicated I felt I had been used and did not like it. "There was no need to go through all the pretense of wanting to date me. All you had to do was tell me what you had in mind and ask if I would be willing to do it. But no, you did it under false pretenses."

"I didn't want to take the chance you'd say 'no,'" he said dismissively.

When I foolishly mentioned this to my father, he typically said he thought what Howard had done was complimentary to me, "You should be flattered." It was no surprise that my father didn't see it as disrespectful and manipulative.

So when Tully instructed me to wear my dress, hat, and gloves, I chafed, inquiring, "Are we going to a ceremony of some kind?"

"No. We're going to church. I want you to meet my preacher." He was telling me what I should wear to church.

Meet his preacher? I could feel my stomach descend to around my knees. Everything was getting worse by the moment. I was being encased in the sticky silken threads of a spider's web of committed emotional expectation. So early that Sunday morning the whole family piled into the car. Acting like a nervous bridegroom awaiting my veiled-in-white entrance down the aisle, he enthusiastically introduced me to his minister after the service. He must have previously talked with him because the man of the cloth put Tully and my hands together and raised his hand as if to bless this union. I swallowed hard and wanted to pull my hand away. All I could think was that I had better find a hefty branch to grab ASAP before the quicksand started to pull me under and drown me.

That afternoon we drove to Oxford to the University of Mississippi to see the Rebels play. Tully wore his Ole Miss Yale blue and crimson cap and his team won. Ole Miss, like Baylor, had a bear as mascot. Sunday evening when he drove me back to the airport, he chattered happily about our starting our life together.

"I'm glad you came to meet Ma and my brothers, my minister, and all my friends. I know they're as crazy about you as I am."

Feeling my heart turn cold and black, I knew I had to drop the bomb on him now. Either that or "disappear" once I returned to Massachusetts but I didn't want to play a game of hide-and-seek with him. Unable to sleep Saturday night, I struggled to conjure up some reasonable-sounding story, such as: My ex-boyfriend who had gone to Vietnam as an officer had been thought to have been killed in action. Miraculously he had survived but just barely. Badly wounded, he had been shipped back to the States and was currently in the hospital. When he couldn't reach me, he had called my mother to let her know he wanted to see me, to ask if we could try again if he made it.

Tully's face screwed up with anger, unfathomable hurt, and humiliation. With his emotions accelerating, he retorted, "I knew there was someone else. How could you do this? How could you string me along? I brought you down here to meet my family and friends and preacher because we were going to be together ... forever." And now, I was telling him this? I had destroyed his dream. There was obviously a special place in hell for people like me.

Quickly I explained, trying to look as guilty and remorseful as I felt, "I didn't know until my mother told me when I called her this afternoon to tell her when to pick me up at the airport. She had received his call this morning and was shocked to hear from him. After what he's been through, I have to at least see him to discuss it."

His face red with pain and eyes wet, accusing me of the worst kind of betrayal, he abruptly left me at the flight gate to return to his car and the unquenchable mortification of my rejection of his love. After all his sharing, planning, and preparation, I had coldly given him a "Dear John" letter ... and worst of all, I had done it in person. *If only* I had known how to handle such a potentially-heart-butchering situation before it had evolved as far as it had.

* *

Resulting Awareness: Letting him win after I had continually said "no" about my visiting, I was rewarding him for being persistent. In his letters the moment I sensed how his perceptions were going, I should have indicated I felt there might be an emotional commitment on his part then explained that I didn't share it. Then if it continued, I should have put my foot down on the phone and sent back his ticket. The made-up story was really unnecessary for me because I didn't need to have an excuse. But perhaps it was necessary for

Tully to help him save some face in this terrible situation we both had created.

The question I asked myself: How else could I have stepped back from his emotion and my unassertiveness to rationally assess the situation and then assertively respond in a timely fashion?

* * *

11

JESSIE

A few who wrote me came across as terribly needy. Jessie, who was a super-patriot from Georgia, had been wounded five times, receiving five separate Purple Hearts for his having habitually been made into a slice of Swiss cheese. Unlike my other correspondents, he wrote twice a day, each letter being several pages, using both sides but he didn't include a photograph. Almost immediately opening his heart to me, he bared his soul. He revealed his sad, insecure, and bullied, early life which seemed to play some role in his being a continuous target. He also agonized over his moral conflict with killing women and children, our dropping napalm on human beings, and contending with the smell of human flesh and gun powder burning in the morning with his coffee. As one who considered himself so gung-ho, these contradictions were eating him alive. They were making him less focused on what he had to do there, and putting him in even graver danger.

Everything about him struck me as traumatized, depressed, and potentially self-destructive ... beyond his obliviously already sporting a bull's eye for the enemy. His past relationships with women had left him bereft, wondering if he were lovable, and fearing he would never find someone who would really care for him. Then the expected sadly occurred.

He likewise had decided we had been "blessed by and united under God." We would be married and live together at

Fort Benning, near Columbus, Georgia, where he was returning to be hospitalized after his very last bullet-ventilation. Fort Benning was where they had the Scout dog school for training dogs to detect ambushes in enemy terrain. Jessie hoped that if he couldn't go back into battle, which was likely at this point, he could get involved in the dogs' initial training before they were transferred to Vietnam for their further advanced courses. In detail he described for me where our married housing would be, what it looked like, and how we could decorate it.

I felt so guilty, wondering if I hadn't been working days and going to school nights, if I might have spotted this early and finally found a way to address it before it developed to this point. But, in reality, I knew down deep that unless I simply stopped writing, this was a forgone conclusion from letter one.

He needed someone desperately—someone who truly cared. I had been kind, interested, and respectful. Maybe I was the only one who ever had been that way. Or, more likely, maybe his circumstance simply acted as a magnifying lens through which he saw only an exaggerated, ideal picture of me. To him, and only a couple of others, my kindness, interest, and respect meant love. I was the "one" and I was stuck ... again.

I puzzled long and hard about how I was going to let him down. Anyone who had his background and conflicts and repeatedly spent that much time in the hospital was emotionally fragile. He had chosen, almost literally, to put his life in my hands. What this meant was that no matter what I said, how kindly, tenderly, and empathetically I expressed it, my "rejection" was going to hurt him badly. Perhaps I had been short-sighted but I hadn't bargained on this kind of responsibility when I offered to write my letters.

The only thing I could think of was to lie again. I didn't want Jessie to feel I was rejecting him because of anything personal he had shared with me about himself. He already felt bad enough about himself without my help adding to it. Even in these extreme circumstances, lying to these individuals made me writhe with guilt.

After his having emotionally arranged our future together, he finally sent me a photo of himself. Now I felt even worse. He was African-American. A lightning bolt struck me. I cringed as I thought that he had not sent me a picture of himself immediately because he feared my initial rejection. So he put it off as long as possible. And now, after he had sent the picture along with his marriage plan, he would no doubt think I was rejecting him because of his skin color.

I used my ex-boyfriend ploy anyway. If there had been a more merciful choice, I was more than eager to hear it. But rejection was still cold, soul-killing rejection. Sometimes it seemed I couldn't do anything right with respect to how they perceived and responded to my letters. It was my fervent hope that Jessie survived his mental anguish, physical wounds, and my rejection to find someone who could and would love him. I never heard from him again and feared the worst for him.

* *

Resulting Awareness: Even if I could have been more sensitive to what his letters were telling me on a gut level, I'm not confident that addressing it immediately would have been the right thing to do in his situation. I felt he had determined that my letters were keeping him functioning, somewhat less depressed and suicidal, and getting the job done. They may have actually helped him to make it back to the States alive.

The question I asked myself: What could I have done given the constraints of war and correspondence that would have helped him without leading him on or getting me too psychologically involved?

* * *

MARK

In his late twenties, Mark was from Connecticut. Every letter he sent he typed. In the first one he stated, "You should not be insulted by my typing this letter to you. I type everything. I can express myself on paper better and much faster that way. Besides, my handwriting is illegible. If you don't like it, we don't have to write." That took me aback as being unnecessarily hostile. Was that a result of combat or how he responded in general?

From his articulate two-page, single-spaced first letter I could see he was well-educated, intelligent, with numerous interests. However, some of the letters that followed were so full of general rage and violent language that I had difficulty reading them. Some described horrific scenarios. One in particular revealed a shocking dimension of modern war that he and my other correspondents were experiencing that I had never conceived. In one such incident a member of his platoon had gone haywire one evening, perhaps from smoking too much pot, lack of sleep, and the untenable, unending stress of strangers lurking everywhere wanting to kill you. Running around camp, screaming, thus inadvertently letting the enemy know their precise position, he was pulling the pins out of hand grenades to try to "frag" the officers in their tents. Mark was one of the officers at the time. Mark put it very succinctly, "Fighting the Viet Cong is not our only danger here. You never know when you are going to receive a bullet in the back of your head or a piece of shrapnel from a fellow soldier who has gone out of his fucking mind"

While I could certainly understand some of his anger, the twenty-nine others who wrote to me managed to modulate their negative emotions in their letters. In fact, even Tully and Jessie had been generally positive in spite of everything. I felt there had to be something else going on adding fuel to Mark's raging inferno. In telling me about himself, he mentioned his fractured family, his early writing for the New York stage, and his traumatically messy divorce which had been initiated while he was in action in Vietnam. His "Dear John" letter apparently had given him a focus in an undercurrent of unrelenting anger—that same anger he poured out to me. Almost as a contradiction, the pictures of himself he had sent showed him smiling, looking relaxed. As a result, when he mentioned getting back to the States and meeting me, I felt conflicted. At least there was practically no chance of his misinterpreting my letters to mean any manner of emotional commitment.

My letters to him were different from my letters to the other twenty-nine. Because he and I appeared at first blush to have a great deal in common, I joked, shared puns, political commentary, movie, book, and theater reviews with him. I philosophized about various issues while keeping it lighter than I would with someone not in his situation. I included various newspaper articles that could be used as a springboard for conversations or give him something to read when not under fire. So when he dropped me a letter to say he was back in the States and still desirous of seeing me, I was somewhat interested despite his overarching anger.

He was in Massachusetts visiting his brother so we made a date to meet at a restaurant in Weston, north of Wellesley, on Route 20, the old Boston Post Road. It was a balmy, clear night, the sky glutted with coruscations of silver paper stars pasted on a navy blue crepe paper background. I dressed in a dark reddish-brown long vest with gold buttons and a matching straight skirt, a gold-colored artist's blouse with long, flowing sleeves, stockings, and beige high heels. My waist-length hair was gently waved and cascading down my back. Attired in crisp chinos and a carefully pressed short-sleeve shirt, he was indeed as attractive and polished-looking in person as in his photo.

Though dinner went smoothly enough with our conversing continuously over our meal, something was amiss. He seemed very reserved, distant. It was something I wasn't sure how to interpret and deal with. Was this an expected reflection of his recent negative experiences? Or was this his reaction specifically to me in person?

Because of his seeming detachment, I tried to match his lower-key energy level. If he were having an adjustment problem getting back into civilian life, maybe even experiencing post-traumatic stress disorder or depression, I didn't want to come across as too funny, happy-go-lucky, or off-the-wall. Even though I had shared elements of those in my letters, I didn't want to perhaps appear insensitive to where he was coming from. Then after having initially met him where he seemed to be emotionally, I then tried to slowly get him to mirror my more positive, upbeat behaviors as I increased my energy level. But strangely it wasn't working. He seemed elsewhere.

When we finished and walked out of the restaurant, I could see things had not only not improved but also were sinking fast. Since I have always hated to leave a problem unresolved, I suggested, as a last resort, that we take a walk around a small grassy park-like stretch nearby. A part of Weston College land where Merriam Road diverged from Concord Road, it was a short distance from Boston College's Weston College Observatory. This was a geophysical research laboratory which housed the World-Wide Standardized Seismic Network.

Even as I drove us there, an uncomfortable silence prevailed. Nothing had changed by the time we had pulled off Concord Road. Surrounded by trees, the area was tranquilly seductive, begging us to walk its soothing confines. As we were strolling slowly across it, I was still trying to draw him out but wondering why I was continuing to bother. Finally I said to myself with a sigh, "I am sick of this. If he wants to remain dyspeptic, so be it. I'm going to enjoy being here. He can choose to like it or not. At this point I don't really care."

With that, I took off my high heels and ran laughing through the grass in my stocking feet, gamboling in a meadow like a spring lamb. My feet were getting wet but it didn't matter because the grass was cool and very refreshing. My engaging with Nature was the only thing about this evening I enjoyed. Despite the tasty dinner, this date had been a huge waste of my time and emotional effort.

To my wonderment Mark loped after me. His demeanor had done a one-eighty. He was smiling. What he said next shocked me. "You know, I was thinking of leaving you flat, never to see you again. You seemed too reserved and conservative for my taste. That was until you took your shoes off and ran through the grass. It was then I decided I'd give you a second chance."

Stunned, I rolled his words around in my head. He was going to give *me* a second chance? That nearly bowled me over. I had been walking around potential land mines all evening, repeatedly giving *him* the benefit of the doubt. The very least I thought he could do was reciprocate. His statement did not give me a warm, fuzzy feeling about him He hadn't even considered giving me the benefit of the doubt about my in-person presentation not matching what he had seen through my letters? Just a "so long, see you around?" The more I massaged his words, the more they really annoyed me.

Since he finally had given me his "seal of approval," he indicated he would ask me for another date or two before he returned to Connecticut. I suspected he wouldn't have been all that distressed if I didn't go out with him again. Still, I wondered where the wit, charm, and cleverness I had felt lurking under all that anger in his writing were, if they could percolate to the surface again, this time in person.

I did see him again twice, but each subsequent date brought with it his judgments about his wife. He had moments of wit and charm but they tended to be superseded by his anger with his ex-wife, about whom he frequently railed. In addition, he seemed defensive, not wanting to be judged, negatively evaluated, or perceived as wrong in any way. That was not going to diminish any time soon. The war apparently had only amplified his problems. All in all, after the third date, I was not willing to continue to experience his rapid emotional cycling, egotistic flare ups, and ongoing hostility. We parted company amicably.

After he left, he sent me a postcard. On the front was the Gestalt Prayer by humanistic psychologist Fritz Perls from *Gestalt Therapy Verbatim*: "I do my thing and you do your thing. I am not in this world to live up to your expectations, and you are not in this world to live up to mine. You are you, and I am I, and if by chance we find each other, it's beautiful. If not, it can't be helped." While I agreed with the sentiment and psychology behind it, I wasn't sure what Mark was saying to me in using it. Then in the message block on the back he wrote a lyric from Carole King's song, "It's Going to Take Some Time": "It's one more round for experience and I'm one the road again." That struck me as disdainful. But at least his thinking he loved me was the farthest thing from his mind.

* *

Resulting Awareness: Meeting with Mark was more from a sense of my own desperation for a relationship than thinking we were truly simpatico. But an even stronger component was, perhaps, reconnecting with the familiar aspects of my childhood, specifically anger. Everything in my family was done out of and through anger with a side helping of insecurity and low self-esteem. Even though I recognized now that I could no longer tolerate the constant pain and stress I used to have to endure, I still had a lingering unconscious allegiance to it.

The question I asked myself: What other unhealthy behavior and relationship patterns did I still have loyalty to that I needed to change?

* * *

Signe A. Dayhoff, PhD

California

Now living in San Diego on Arizona Street, just off University, I was continuing to have difficult interactions with men. Most of these encounters occurred as a result of my attending weekly Saturday singles' dances at the El Cortez Hotel. The hotel, which was the tallest building in San Diego at the time, sat impressively atop a hill at the north end of the city. During the late 1960s and 1970s, the El Cortez was falling on hard times and in decline after which it closed. Then later, after I had left California, the El Cortez was finally sold to Morris Cerullo, an Assemblies of God minister, to become a school of evangelism. It was he who also purchased Heritage USA, the Christian theme park in South Carolina, from TV evangelist Jim Bakker. Many years thereafter, the El Cortez became an historic landmark, ultimately becoming what it is today: a prized location for condominiums, lofts, penthouses, luxury apartments, commercial and office space.

There we danced to records of all the latest tunes as well as old standards. Always loving to dance, I took full advantage of these occasions to meet men while enjoying the physicality and artistry of expressing myself to music. While some attendees could dance very well, some polkaed or clogged in time to foxtrots, waltzes, and rumbas. And some were obviously unaware that ballroom dancing was supposed to involve following some pre-determined patterns of foot placement and matching them to the music's rhythm. Consequently, it was those individuals who hokey-pokey-ed, race-walked, or bunny-hopped their way around the floor, ultimately stomping on my feet, sacrificing more than one pair of stockings to the Florsheim Gods.

* * *

13

FRED

The age range of those men attending was broad, from mid-twenties to the forties. There was one man who was much older than most of the other dancers. A good technical dancer, he was tall, thin, and raw-boned. When I foxtrotted with him, however, he felt all tight muscles, tendons, and sinews rather than grace in motion. Perhaps sensing my awareness of these prominent anatomical features, he made a point of telling me he was a runner. It seemed important that he assure me that his body was all knotted because of marathon training and not because of his "advancing" age. Everything about fiftyish Fred made him seem like a too tightly wound alarm clock spring.

He had a tendency to crowd out the other men who wanted to dance with me. In spite of that being complimentary, he was messing up the other prong of my plan for being there. "Fred," I said smiling, "you need to give the other women a chance to dance with you since you're such a smooth dancer." When that didn't work, I resorted to, "Fred, I need to give the other men a chance to dance with me since I'm such a smooth dancer." The latter tended to work better than the former. Then one evening he offered to drive me home.

"That's very nice, Fred, but I have my car."

"But I want to show you my etchings on the way."

I looked at him with a jaundiced eye, "Etchings, Fred, really?" I almost added, "That ploy went out with high-button shoes," but stopped in time since he was obviously self-conscious about his age.

"Yes, I really do have etchings. What? Do you think I am trying to lure you to my apartment to take advantage of you?"

"Well, yes, maybe," I laughed. "But if you truly do have them and want to show them to me, that's fine. However, if there is anything else on your mind ... uh-uh-uh." I wagged my finger dramatically at him.

"Would I do that?" I raised my eyebrows. "Not to worry," he grinned.

I followed him in my car. His apartment was on University, not all that far from the apartment I shared with my mother. She generally joined me at the dances since she was her own Ginger Rogers. Mother echoed Ginger's belief that she could do and did do anything a "Fred Astaire" did but did it better because she had to "do it backwards and in high heels." But this evening she had had to place some calls to the East Coast instead.

When we arrived at his apartment complex, we walked into the patio which was colorfully designed with pygmy date palms, mandevilla, hibiscus, bougainvillea, and bird of paradise around the perimeter with a large aquamarine swimming pool in the center. From there he pointed out his apartment on the second floor. Before I had a chance to even nod in acknowledgment, he grabbed me, sweeping me up into his tightly-muscled arms. Without a moment's hesitation he ran up the two flights of exterior stairs.

Granted at five-three and one hundred two pounds I was not a large or heavy load to carry upstairs, but running up the stairs with me? I didn't know whether I was more afraid he would drop me on the stairs or he would have a

Attracting and Dating the Wrong Men?

heart attack before he reached his apartment door ... and then drop me over the wrought iron railing to the cement below. I hung on for dear life. At the top of the second flight of stairs, his heart was racing faster than I could count with my ear near his thinly-muscled chest. Dear Lord, I thought, don't let it be atrial fibrillation because I don't carry a portable defibrillator in my handbag.

Apparently he felt that he had to demonstrate unequivocally that while he may have been a little long in the tooth, he was still a force to be reckoned with. Moreover, a "young thing like me" shouldn't let a man's "golden-age maturity" stand in the way of a budding "true romance." Despite what I was sure was incipient apoplexy covering his face and neck in a deepening purple, he looked at me in a way suggesting he was about to take me into my bower where he would ravish me, with us spending long hours in violin-accompanied bliss.

Even before he tried to recapture his breath, he bent down to give me a big kiss as he fitted his key into the door lock. I was only partially successful in blocking his oxygen-starved passion. Once inside his door, I saw he did indeed have etchings framed on the walls. However, this was not the Guggenheim and it was obvious he had not brought me here for a museum or gallery tour. I wanted to head home before any other ideas occurred to him while I was still within arm's reach. He had proved to me that he was not the least bit geriatric. Perhaps that was enough for this evening. Since I continued to indicate I wasn't "available" for any other of his desired activities, he good-naturedly let me go home, without the sweeping violins.

* *

Resulting Awareness: I was getting stronger, more independent, and more assertive with men in general and with those who were older. Age was becoming less of a connection to my father. The more uncomplicated the situation, the more assertive I was becoming.

The question I asked myself: How could I expand on my assertiveness?

* * *

14

JOHN

Another dancer, John, who was in his early thirties, ran a fried chicken franchise. He was no bunny-hopper, race-walker, or hokey-pokey-er. We delightfully tripped the light fantastic together often at each dance, dancing as one. One evening after we had finished a set, he said, "Hey, maybe we could team up. You know, enter dance contests together. There are lots of contests nationally. It's a coming trend."

I had never thought of becoming a ballroom dancer and he was talking about it as more than a hobby. If I had wanted a dance career, I would have trained to dance on Broadway or with a great dance company, like that of Martha Graham, Alvin Ailey, or Paul Taylor. But John seemed particularly serious about becoming a ballroom dancer now that he felt he had a partner with whom he was comfortable.

Dancing for me was a leisurely fun activity. I couldn't imagine going from town to town, entering one contest after another, as we moved around the country. It had a tacky, exhausting aspect to it that didn't appeal to me, like being with a band on the road going from gig to gig to gig. It suddenly reminded me of Sydney Pollack's dark film, *They Shoot Horses, Don't They?* It is about marathon dancing for fraudulently non-existent prizes with Gig Young as the sleazy, lying Master of Ceremonies saying, "Yowza, yowza!" from minstrel show infamy, until the contestants dropped, dropped dead, or quit.

Once I decided, I let John know of my limited interest. We could practice together and if there were a contest in San Diego to enter, fine—otherwise, no. Even though he agreed, he seemed to hold onto the dream of our someday dancing in competition on television at the Harvest Moon Ball Dance Championships. We met occasionally to try new steps or new dances. When we did, it was most often at his apartment because it had a room with a bare wood floor. Most apartments, like mine, were fully carpeted. However, it wasn't long before his male mind started to wander to more horizontal activities.

One afternoon after we had spent an hour inelegantly practicing the tango, he was to drive me home. My car had to be in the shop for several hours that day to fix an exhaust problem. However, no sooner had we entered his car in his apartment complex parking lot than he decided it was that time to single-handedly consummate our relationship. It was "Damn the torpedoes, full-steam ahead." Tightly gripping my shoulders and twisting the right one, he tried to shove me down on the front bench seat of his 1958 Chevy.

I shouted. "Stop! Get off me! What do you think you trying to do! Owww. You're hurting my shoulder. Let go of me! S-t-o-p!!!"

In his testosterone-precipitated fog, my words were unheard, being steamrolled by his deafening passion. Despite my fists flailing, barely missing his face, he struggled to render my upper torso supine. I was determined this was not going to happen. But he was just as determined that it was ... and my right shoulder was caught in the crossfire. Anger was pumping gallons of adrenaline into my body as I continued to shout "Stop!"

Ten minutes passed before my physical and verbal resistance began to penetrate his cranium, creating a small awareness that perhaps I was not acting like a "consenting adult" after all. The wrestling subsided. My right shoulder screamed with pain and felt anatomically misaligned. Very carefully attempting to stretch and rotate it, I was thankful to discover that my arm actually had not been wrenched out of its socket, as I had suspected during the melee, no thanks to John.

John looked a little contrite. He said, sheepishly, "I thought you wanted it."

"You thought what? You thought I wanted it? What? A dislocated shoulder? Didn't my shouting 'NO' and 'Stop' give you a clue that I wasn't asking to be mauled?"

"Well, maybe, I don't know. I thought you might be playing games. You know how some women say 'no' when they mean 'yes.' And some want a little fight, maybe a little pain. I was only responding to the signals you were sending me."

"*My* signals? What in heaven's name *are* you talking about?"

"When we danced, you were pressing your boobs against me."

"You can't be serious! We were doing the tango for godssake! Bodies touch when people dance! That doesn't mean I want you to try to assault me."

"But ... I thought ... I don't know. How am I supposed to know?"

"When in doubt, ask!"

"Okay, well, I guess I made a mistake."

I rolled my eyes. "You sure did! If a woman says 'no,' take it to mean 'no.'" I rotated my arm again, grimacing. "I don't want to continue our dancing practice. In fact," I paused as it occurred to me, "I'm not sure I want us to dance even at the El Cortez if you're going to interpret any body contact as a sexual invitation." He remained silent.

The next morning, before he opened his fast-food restaurant, he drove over to my apartment. If he had had a hat, it would have been in his hands with his head hanging low. Standing outside my second-floor apartment door, he said, "I'm sorry I hurt your shoulder. I didn't mean to. I want you to have this as an apology."

From behind his back he brought forth a white store box which he handed to me. In it were ten pieces of his hot, greasy fried chicken drumsticks. I thanked him without the look of amazement that was trying to creep into my expression. "I'll see you at the El Cortez," he said glancing into my eyes momentarily, before looking down again and descending the outside apartment building stairs. Shaking my head, I considered having the chicken parts bronzed and mounted with a brass plate to memorialize this once-in-a-lifetime apology.

* *

Resulting Awareness: I found myself becoming ambivalent about my interactions with men. Most of the men I encountered seemed to revel in a shallow perception of relationships with women: "Don't sweat it. There'll be another along in a minute."

The question I asked myself: How could I achieve a happy medium with attraction and dating men so I could avoid both disdain and serious commitment?

* * *

15

TIM

At the El Cortez I met a court reporter, named Tim. Tall, dark, and chunky, he was always trying to impress me with how intelligent and knowledgeable he was by creating word definitions and philosophizing about what he considered to be "deep" ideas. I had seen him going around with Julie, who also was always present at the singles' dances. Attractive and petite, she was divorced and had a young son. In spite of their having seemed to be a couple, Tim invited me to attend his church of Religious Science the next Sunday then go for a walk. I wondered if that meant they weren't going together any longer. I accepted his invitation even though I quickly found he never ceased smelling of cigarettes and stale coffee which reminded me of a New York City subway car.

At that time I had never heard of "religious science." It sounded like an oxymoron to me. As I sat in the pew next to Tim in the spacious but crowded modern church, the minister talked about the power of belief. Tim seemed enrapt. According to the minister, if a plane had a mechanical problem that guaranteed a crash but all the passengers truly, positively believed it wouldn't crash, the plane wouldn't crash. However, if the plane crashed, it was because someone either didn't believe or didn't believe hard enough. Tim found the concept inspiring. "You can achieve *anything* if you believe hard enough. Isn't that amazing?"

Because my science background, I saw what he found to be miraculous as something that was simply un-provable. "Tim, how is one supposed to be able to measure what 'enough belief' is in order to make it happen?"

Tim waved his hand to disregard my question. "It's a matter of believing, having faith. You can't measure belief."

"But you just said—." I stopped there. This was one of those arguments that could go nowhere. "So, where should we walk?"

"I thought we could go to Balboa Park but I have to stop by my apartment first."

I hoped this was not another half-witted attempt at seduction which I'd found to be so popular in San Diego. Tim's studio apartment had clothes strewn everywhere. In spite of that, it looked to have been cleaned sometime recently ... except for the bed. The bed was another story. Unmade, it had sheets that evidenced a lot of action. Many stains and different colored pubic hairs decorated them. Even *if* I had been interested in a roll in the hay with Tim, which I wasn't, his bed would have been a real turn off.

Tim saw me looking at the bed and commented, "Oh, yeah, Julie hasn't been by in the last couple of days to change the sheets."

"Change the sheets?"

"Yeah, when we're not getting it on, she cleans my apartment for me and does my laundry."

"For pay, I hope."

"Don't be silly."

I wondered whether Julie was that desperate for male companionship and a potential dad for her child that she was willing to do *everything* for Tim a wife would do but without the license. Of course, it was possible she just enjoyed cleaning and doing laundry so much that she sought it out at every opportunity.

Attracting and Dating the Wrong Men?

After we explored only one of Balboa Park's one thousand acres, touring the rose and desert gardens, Tim offered to buy me lunch. I was thinking a salad and some iced tea might be nice on this hot, sunny day in an air-conditioned restaurant.

However, we "dined" upright at a hot-dog stand. To enhance the *al fresco* experience the mustard acted like Mt. Vesuvius spewing yellow lava haphazardly from its partially-plugged condiment squeeze bottle. Its droplets decorated my blouse which Tim "graciously" volunteered to lick off for me. Last of the big spenders, Tim then suggested we go back to his apartment for a little "relaxation."

"The bed won't have been made but we won't notice."

I said, "Thanks but no thanks," trying to cover my rolling burp from the nitrate infused lump of pig snout on a bun. I left him to Julie and her free maid service.

* *

Resulting Awareness: I was going out less frequently and going with men in whom I had little interest because it seemed there was a great deal of insecurity and pretension in those who asked me out. Interestingly, I found I was beginning to mirror that insecurity despite my increasing degree of assertiveness. Too many of these men reminded me of my father and his expectations of what females were and what they should do.

The question I asked myself: Was it better not to go out at all to avoid frustration than to go out and learn how to deal with their individual and collective idiosyncrasies despite all the annoyance?

* * *

# 16

TOM

Over the course of seven months of dances at the El Cortez, I developed a pure-and-chaste-from-afar crush on a very popular dancer whose look and lithe, graceful movements seduced every woman on the dance floor. Short, athletic, with wheat-colored hair, and hazel eyes, Tom exuded animal magnetism. I loved the lighter-than-air feeling of dancing on winged feet which I always experienced with him. He was so subtly sexual that his come-hither moves made him all the more attractive. I had long since given up the idea of his ever showing interest in me other than as a dance partner and decided that that alone was worth settling for.

Then, unexpectedly, one evening he asked me to go for coffee. I was nearly speechless. I wondered what could have changed to precipitate that invitation. Coffee was potentially a good step, giving us both more information with which to work. Then to my disbelieving ears he further suggested going to his apartment. Things were not only moving but also moving fast—perhaps too fast. Despite my less than stellar experiences with men's apartments, I convinced myself things were not only okay but sounding better and better. It was clear he had come to recognize that I was an interesting person, not merely a good dance partner, and wanted to get to know me better. Strangers things than that had happened. If he only knew how long I had hoped for his invitation.

Attracting and Dating the Wrong Men?

Good fortune was smiling on me and I felt on top of the world. I was as giddy as a little girl receiving her first Valentine from the little boy who shyly smiled at her on the playground. This reminded me that good things do happen to good people. Before I got into my car to follow him, he off-handedly said, "On second thought, let's have coffee at my place instead."

While I would have preferred a coffee shop first, coffee at his apartment would be okay. I responded casually, "Sure," but inside I was shouting, "Go, team, go!" cheering my first touchdown in this All-Star game. What would his apartment be like and what might it tell me about him? That reminded me how very little I actually knew about him. I didn't know what he did for a living, where he came from, or what his interests were besides dancing. He rarely spoke while dancing, focusing on his perfect moves and creating a sympathetic chord between us. Now would be the chance to fill in the gaps that I had been optimistically assuming all along reflected our many similarities. Then, after we got to know each other a bit better, I hoped we'd also take a little time to "make out."

When we arrived, I was surprised to see how dull-looking his three-room apartment was. There were no pictures on the wall. No books decorating a bookcase or table. No athletic equipment piled against the wall. At least it was neat and looked relatively clean. Immediately he made coffee. I found out he was from Ohio and in sales of medical equipment. Then after the etiquette-required preliminaries, things then began to speed up and heat up. We started to make out on his forest green piped cotton spread-covered day bed, which was pushed against the right-hand wall. A lot of preliminary grappling was taking place in a shorter time than I had expected but I was thrilled he seemed to like me as much as I liked him. Our caressing, kissing, minor fondling, and petting seemed to reflect his enthusiasm.

Just then the phone rang. I was startled but Tom was grinning. I couldn't tell if he was grinning because of our activity or he was expecting the call. As he spoke on the phone, he stared at me, occasionally laughing. Soon he began to describe in exquisitely graphic detail what he had been doing to me on the daybed—specifically where he had put his hands, how, and when. "I was about to unbutton her third button and slip my fingers inside, to slide down her chest, approach her bra where I was going to finger her breasts and make my way to tickling her nipples."

In my disheveled but dressed state, I was sitting on the daybed, staring at him, disbelieving, immobilized by my extreme embarrassment at what he was saying ... about me ... and what he wanted to do to me! My mind couldn't quite wrap itself about the craziness that was happening. It felt like a scene out of the dark psychological horror-thriller, *Repulsion*, where we watch Catherine Deneuve slowly, unemotionally descend into schizophrenic hallucinations and derangement.

Before I could get up, he began to further detail all my moves and my physical and emotional responses to what he was doing. "She was breathing more heavily, sweating, and wriggling and squirming under my touch, enjoying herself. Her hair is messed up and she looks as if she's been snagged and tagged but is definitely none the worse for it." He laughed loudly and handed the phone to me. In my hypnotic state I took it. On the other end of the line was his male friend. He was laughing too. It suddenly became clear. I had been the object of some calculated game by which they were mutually mentally masturbating. My expressions of anger were barely a squeak above my humiliation. Quickly I straightened my skirt and blouse, put on my shoes, and left without a word or a look at him.

After being treated like a *Penthouse* magazine for spanking the monkey or some sadistic purpose, I wondered how many other women had experienced this demeaning behavior with him. As a result, I decided never to go to the dances again. Part of me wanted to go and ignore him, letting him know his sophomoric high-school actions hadn't fazed me one bit. But at the time I didn't feel brave enough to meet his eyes and read what I was sure he was thinking behind that knowing smile.

I let him control my emotions and behavior. In doing so, I cut myself off from something I enjoyed immensely and that gave me expression. I gave my power away. Moreover, I helped him enhance his own power through my lack of confidence and assertiveness.

* *

Resulting Awareness: In a moment of desperation I had disregarded lots of intuition-related signs that suggested this would not be a person with whom to go out. He never seemed close to anyone or all that friendly. I never saw him with women except when he was dancing with them. Moreover, there was always a distance between us even when dancing that I had chosen to ignore. His suddenly asking me out made no logical or emotional sense.

The question I asked myself: What could I learn from this experience and how could I use it to benefit myself now and in the future?

* * *

17

RANDALL

All the time I was living in San Diego, I was working at Scripps Clinic and Research Foundation in La Jolla. La Jolla was the affluent, hilly seaside "jewel" of a community occupying seven miles of curving Pacific coastline. It was a short thirty minutes north of San Diego off Interstate 5. Though I was involved in the paperwork for the Upjohn Double-Blind Diabetes Medication Study, under the aegis of Dr. Lambert, head of the Metabolic Disease Department there, I often chanced to meet the general patients that Dr. Lambert also saw.

One such person was John Wayne, who, like other film stars, was sent by the movie studios in Los Angeles for his annual physicals or specific health problems. My chance observation of him was particularly memorable. He was walking down the clinic hallway from Dr. Lambert's office with his signature rolling gait wearing nothing but a pale blue hospital johnny. Because his six-foot-four frame made the gown way too short for him, he was constantly tugging on it to make it at least partially cover his private parts. In his wake, as he walked back to his room, came a stream of invectives, ending with, "Oh, shit!"

One morning as I was collating data in Dr. Lambert's outer office, a thirtyish "Michael Corleone"-type from the *Godfather,* walked toward Lambert's office. With his precisely trimmed and carefully-styled, blow-dried and sprayed dark hair, he was dressed in a gray three-piece suit with a black shirt and black tie. He was dashing in a gangster-like way. There wasn't much question that he was someone who wanted to effect that "bad boy" image. While he carried himself erect, his walk suggested the impertinence of a slight swagger.

Being unlike the men to whom I was usually exposed, I found him a little intriguing even though he was no Al Pacino. As he was leaving Lambert's inner office, we glanced at one another. He gave me a small smile and lowered his lids. It was obvious he wanted me to notice his dark lashes that contrasted with his robin's egg blue eyes. He paused, "I'm Randall Antony. When do you get a break?" Oily words were pouring smoothly from his lips like suet melting in the sun. "I'll be here most of the day and thought we might get to know each other."

I looked at my watch, asking myself if I wanted to do something different and spur of the moment. Thinking "why not," I said, "I'm off to lunch in fifteen minutes. What do you have in mind?"

"We can check out the local bistros. I'll wait for you in the hall." He leaned against the door jamb and shoved his right hand into his front pants pocket. From his pose I expected him to pull out a quarter and start flipping the coin like George Raft's gangster "Guino Rinaldo" in the original 1932 *Scarface*.

Fifteen minutes later we were walking up the sidewalk on Prospect Place north to a delicatessen for Reuben sandwiches. Taking control of the conversation, he shared with me he was an aeronautical engineer working on defense logistics in Costa Mesa, living in Irvine, was married but separated, and played pool professionally. "I was referred to Scripps because of blinding headaches and severe stomach pains. I'm scheduled for gastrointestinal and neurological tests and a psychiatric consultation."

I could easily envision him as a pool sharp, luring guileless flies into his spider's web, easily picking them off one by one, fleecing them of the money that they were practically begging him to take. Everything about him projected his sense of his own superiority in his skills and self-presentation. Apparently he also had no compunction about telling the world that he was an exceptional person who was being thwarted at every turn by those closest to him, that he was the object of hostility and scorn: poor, poor thing.

According to his version of his life circumstances, his wife had not lost the weight she had gained during her pregnancy with their first child fast enough to suit him. He had an image to maintain and she was not cooperating. He admitted he nagged her mercilessly about it. Rather than lose weight, she gained more weight. The more he nagged the more she gained. While this correlation may have slipped by him, it was, perhaps, more likely that he had chosen to use it to add to his sense of victimhood.

He said he hated his wife's father who was an FBI agent. "He's the same as a cop and I can't stand cops. He's all about authority. They think they're always right. He never lets up on me. He constantly has everything I do under a microscope, always looking for anything he can nail me with. It makes me want even more to give him exactly what he wants. You want a bad boy? You got it, Pops, you stupid bastard!" The more he talked about his family and about himself as suffering from their machinations, the more obvious it became that he had significant problems with anger and control.

As he went through his two days of tests and consults at Scripps, we talked on my breaks and at lunch. There was indeed something remotely dangerous about him. But it wasn't so much his implied underworld connections as it was his unstable psychological underpinnings. His life was nothing but emotional turmoil and he didn't know how to handle it except to act out. He was a must to avoid, but I didn't. For the moment he was strangely intriguing. However, when he started calling me after he returned to Irvine, I wasn't sure how I felt about the implications of that.

Several weeks of conversations had gone by when he decided to pay me a visit on the weekend. He arrived early Saturday at my apartment with large florist's box filled with a dozen gardenias. I loved gardenias and had never seen or received so many at one time before. But the gift left me wondering what had prompted his magnanimity. As I was putting the flowers in a bowl of water, he dropped his assumed quid pro quo on me.

Grinning broadly, he said more than asked, "Can I stay here with you?"

"What? No! You can't!"

In exchange for the flowers he expected to stay at my apartment which I shared with my mother. Perhaps I was being naïve, but it had never occurred to me he would try a manipulation so blatant. He was doomed to be disappointed, flowers or not.

"But why not?" he whined with the sound of a two-year-old on the verge of fake crying jag. "I traveled all this way to see you. The least you could do is put me up. It will cost me a lot to get a room somewhere."

"You should have asked me if you could stay here before you came down. If you had, you would have known the answer was 'no.' Just because you assumed you could and came on down doesn't mean I owe you bed and board."

The fragrant gardenias floated languidly in the large, blue-tinted glass bowl I had placed on the slatted walnut coffee table in front of our dark brown Danish-looking sofa. What had been a dazzling "gift" suddenly lost its allure. This manipulation to secure lodgings for him was not something I found remotely endearing. With considerable griping, he secured a room at the Hanalei on Hotel Circle in Mission Hills on Route 5.

That afternoon we found a pool hall in downtown San Diego near the embarcadero. He was intent upon showing me all his professional pool-playing moves. There was no question that he knew his way around a pool table. I was impressed, picking up his tips. Because I played occasionally, I had gotten a cue of my own which I carried in a long, slim black vinyl, zip-up case. Whenever I played, I made a point of striding into the male-dominated pool hall wearing my black leather gloves, removing my two-piece cue, screwing it together, and assuming the "pose" of someone who had an idea about what she was doing.

Because the men there seemed to choose to assume I was some neophyte female player, instead of a hustler looking for suckers, I became an instant magnet. They tripped all over themselves to show the "little lady" a thing or two about the finer points of the masculine art of the game. What was really fun was that even though I was a mediocre player at best, they always managed to rip the green felt covering the slate table or knock the cue ball off onto the floor as testosterone pushed their playing skills off to the side, enabling me to repeatedly win.

The night Randall was to go back to Irvine, he invited me to his hotel room. He had not so delicately intimated he wanted to have sex but I made it clear I wasn't interested. Not one to take "no" for an answer, Randall was pleading, "Aw, come on. Don't be that way. I came all this way to see you. Eighty-seven miles, for godssake! Come on."

"I've told you over and over the answer is 'no.' No means no."

He began to whine again, nothing like his Michael Corleone image, "Just let me put it in. I won't do anything. I promise."

Attracting and Dating the Wrong Men?

If I hadn't been there dealing with a tricky situation ... if I had been watching this play out on the big screen, I would have fallen down on the floor laughing myself silly. Did he really think I'd believe his "I just want to put it in. I won't do anything"?

When it was time to leave, he left in an erection-stifled huff. Ending his visit on that sour note, I thought and hoped I wouldn't see or hear from him again. But, several weeks later, he called, inviting me to Irvine to visit him.

"No, we've said our good-byes. I don't think we should see each other again."

But he coaxed, cajoled, and wheedled. Unfortunately, I still had a problem being as assertive as I wanted. It was as if I still didn't feel I had the right to say "no." Finally I said an angry "yes," but immediately chastised myself for having been so stupid. I knew I had let myself be manipulated by him again. I was sick of letting men bend me to their wills in social situations. I knew I should call him back to cancel. I shouldn't go ... period. He was undoubtedly planning an assignation where he'd want to "put it in" and "*do* something."

Taking the cowardly way out, I asked my mother to come with me as a chaperone. Of course, she did not like Randall. She did not find his "gangster" image cute or appealing. His controlling behaviors reminded her of my father's similar behaviors. Having helped set up a situation of reinforced expectations that weren't going to be met, I wanted backup even though I knew doing this was making a bad situation worse. Given his anger and narcissism, he would have a conniption when he saw I wasn't alone. I should simply not go ... period. Although, I think Mother was actually looking forward to seeing him being one-down and having to deal with it.

When Mother and I arrived in Irvine around noon, Randall came out the kitchen door to greet me. At the sight of two of us he nearly swallowed his tongue. His anger was tangible. For a few minutes he just glared at me. Instead of handling this unexpected situation gracefully, he jutted out his lower lip and totally ignored Mother. He didn't speak to her. He treated her as if she weren't there. I half-expected him to throw himself on the ground, kicking and screaming in his frustration. He was furious with me but couldn't punish me directly because he still hoped he could score. So he did it through my mother. It never seemed to occur to him that his attacking my mother was not going to win my heart physically or in any other way.

It was great fun to watch Mother in this situation though I tried not to outwardly show it. She responded to him with great equanimity and civility as if he hadn't made such a royal horse's rear end out of himself. Confused by our temperate reactions, he moderated his display. I could see he was now rethinking his plan. How could he dispense with my mother for a while so he could work on undressing me? He didn't have to think about that for long because of the explosion.

A thunderous noise erupted from his kitchen. Everyone turned toward his back door, gasping in unison. Cautiously he opened the door. There we were struck in the face by wave of heat from a blast furnace as if someone were pouring molten steel into ingots. The smell of burning rubber choked us. Everywhere there were steaming gray strings of rubber-like material hanging precipitously from the ceiling like Spanish moss, scalding gray pools on the stove top, blistered gray globs glued on the painted white, pine cabinet faces, and still smoldering gray lumps on the countertops and the floor around the stove. The room was a disaster, leaving little room in which to walk around. Randall made his way in, reaching around the sink to throw up the kitchen window as I propped open the outside door. In the shambles of his kitchen, Randall let his anger lapse into perplexity. Slowly it dawned on him what had happened.

Attracting and Dating the Wrong Men?

"Oh, my God, the steak! He opened the oven door to see flames cremating his slab of beef on the broiler pan, gray spatters mixed with grease peppering the inside of the oven. "My steak!" he cried, almost in tears, as he quickly shoved the oven door closed again.

"Wait! You could pull it out and rinse it off. You could still save it." He shook his head "no."

Surveying the kitchen damage, he began to look pitiful. While I had no idea what had transpired, I could tell he knew precisely. "So what happened here?" I asked.

With a deep sigh, he related a long, incredibly sad tale of woe about wanting to broil a steak to have it ready for when I arrived. "The oven door kept closing." With his old-style stove having the oven door shut during broiling was a no-no. However, the hinge that would keep the door ajar was no longer working. "I needed to find something to prop the door open ... you know ... just enough so the broiler would work properly. I mean, you can't broil a steak with the door completely open." He shook his head.

"I tried a bunch of things. You know, hot mitt, wine bottle cork, ball of string, and a bath towel. But nothing really worked. After a while, I thought that a golf ball might do the job. I play golf and could be a pro making a wad of bucks if I wanted."

As I glanced at the cooling gray filaments and accumulations, I thought he ought to finish his recitation soon and get cleaning before it all became permanent kitchen fixtures.

"Anyway, the golf ball was the right size. Its surface even had the right texture to help it stay in place. Then I put the steak in. I set the broiler, placed the golf ball in the corner by the hinge. The door stayed open just the right amount and I waited."

Mother rolled her eyes back in her head. I looked at her, as if to ask, "My God, can you believe this?" and coughed into my hand to stifle the sound of a guffaw.

Immersed in the story, Randall added wistfully, "You could hear the steak sizzling and snapping in there and it smelled great 'cause I had rubbed it down with fresh garlic and Worcestershire sauce. But—then as it was about ready—the damned golf ball must have exploded. Kee-riist! I could have been killed. And the steak is now shit."

He looked around again, the enormity of the scene finally coming into full view. "And now I have crap everywhere. Now what do I do?" It was as if what had happened had left his engineering mind totally bereft about what steps to take next.

"You were lucky to be outside when it happened. You could have been badly burned."

He nodded, looking as if disappointment and appearing doleful were competing for his expression.

"I think you ought to try to get the golf ball innards off everything now, especially your stove."

Leaning toward me, he whispered confidentially, "Could we go out for a while first?" He seemed to think Mother wouldn't hear. He was getting in the mood again, perhaps hoping I'd take pity on him.

"No. This is still a fire hazard."

"Why can't I do it later? Maybe you could help with it then."

"You ought to do it while the stove is still warm and before it solidifies even more. It's probably already hardened on your cabinets, counters, and floors. You'll need a putty knife or glass scraper, rubber gloves, and some kind of rubber solvent."

"Can you do it for me? You seem to know all about cleaning it up. I'm sure you could do it so much better."

"Me? No, sorry. I've never had a golf ball explode. But since you have this mess requiring your immediate attention, I think it would be best if Mother and I don't hold you up any longer. Good luck."

Fortunately I never heard from him again so I never found out if there were solvents specifically for getting melted golf balls off your stove and ceiling. I had heard that different chemicals like formaldehyde, chloroform, toluene, benzene, and aqua regia might possibly work if you don't mind destroying the rubberized, painted, laminated, or varnished surface, your skin, lungs, or your brain. And, if you didn't turn off the stove's pilot light before applying these chemicals, you might destroy your house as well. I wondered what would have happened if he had tried to use a cue-ball instead.

* *

Resulting Awareness: I had allowed myself to follow my old unconscious programming, to become a victim, again, even though it had been obvious to me from the start that a relationship of any kind with this person was rife with problems. Randall could not have been a more "wrong" man to whom to be attracted. Yet I had consciously and purposely put myself in harm's way initially. Then responding unassertively, I couldn't and didn't do what I had to do. I was acting both against and in concert with my childhood allegiance and forbiddances. Even though these were not the best of decisions, which I fully recognized, at least they were my decisions. I was positively stepping out from under my father's expectations.

The question I asked myself: Why was I allowing myself to repeat this behavior pattern even as I became more aware of its existence and disliked it?

* * *

18

BUFF COP

It was a bright, canary-yellow, cloudless day when I was approaching a busy city intersection on foot in National City, about fifteen minutes south from where I lived in San Diego. I was on my way to the public parking garage. I had been to see my gynecologist who was female to get a Pap smear for cervical cancer and check out all the other female essentials. Female physicians tended not to patronize, discount or dismiss what I said or be dogmatic about everything they said as being right and unassailable. Furthermore, they recognized that qualitative information was at least as important as quantitative information. This meant they wanted to know what was going on in your life, physically and emotionally, that might have an impact on your health and well-being.

Today everything looked good. There had been no recurrence of endometrial hyperplasia or the pelvic inflammatory disease, PID, which had plagued me for the last year. My polycystic ovaries had calmed down. And I finally had my frequent urinary infections, which had required surgery earlier on, under control. My doctor had prescribed a daily prophylactic regimen of Macrodantin to prevent another urinary flare-up. This was a nitrofurantoin antibiotic that actually entered the bacterial cell and destroyed its genetic material. It was a boon for me.

Attracting and Dating the Wrong Men?

On the next curb over from my position where I was waiting for the walk sign was a tall, nicely-muscled cop. His dark blue uniform, with the gold patch on his right upper arm, and silver badge on his left breast, fitted every interesting curvature of his buff-looking body. It set off his black wavy hair which I could see when he took his cap off to wipe the sweat off his brow with his hand. His angular facial planes, strong jaw, and quick smiles further piqued my interest. He reminded me of the comic book drawings of Superman. He was talking animatedly to his soggy-in-the-midsection, shirt-gaping partner. This other cop looked as if he had had too many double cheese burgers while sitting in the squad car waiting for the police dispatcher to call with some crime to investigate. In his current condition there was no way he could possibly pursue any suspect on foot for even a block without requiring CPR.

Under the muscular one's shiny black-visored-cap were dark eyebrows which made his at-once-startling gentian baby blues stand out even more. He was a Christopher Reeve as Superman in the flesh, even before Reeve became Superman. If the following expression were to fit anyone, it would fit this gorgeous hunk of masculine flesh. He was, by all definitions, a "stud muffin."

As I started across the intersection, I was moving on a long walk light. This was fortunate because I couldn't take my eyes off him which slowed my pace. How could I get his attention? I wondered. How could I meet him? My mind was a flurry of questions in search of a solution. In general, I was not drawn to gun-toting authority types or muscled men, but in his uniform he looked to be special, definitely a cut above.

I was half-way across the six-lane intersection when ... whomp! I had walked straight into a metal pedestal on a concrete base in the middle of the thoroughfare. My head collided with the large steel sign it was holding. Unceremoniously I was thrown onto my bottom. Seconds slipped by before I started to get my bearings. As I tried to raise my now-bruised body from the asphalt, I slipped again into a sitting position. This had finally gotten the cop's attention. The object of my affection was staring at me with his mouth open. "Hey, lady," he called, "you'd better hurry. The light is going to change."

In my daze I was disappointed he had not run into the street to check on my condition. He didn't have to lift me gently up into his arms and drive away with me in his black-and-white cruiser with all lights flashing to the nearest hospital. But, at least, he could have checked to see if I were hurt or needed assistance. Wasn't he supposed to "protect and serve"?

As I woozily tried again to rise to my feet, a woman on the other side of the street rushed to my aid. "Honey, are you okay. Can you walk? That's a nasty bump you got. Do you think you have a concussion? Should I take you to the ER?"

As my eyes began to focus more clearly, I looked at her, "Uh, no. I ... I think I'm okay." Of course, I had no way of knowing if I were all right. My attention was on the buff cop. Still on his curb, he was glowering at me, motioning me brusquely to get my butt in gear and get off the street.

Grabbing my arm, the woman helped me stand up straight then picked up my handbag which had slipped off my shoulder. The lump on my temple was enlarging, giving me a throbbing headache. When I smashed into the sign, my head had whipped around as well. My neck and shoulder muscles twinged with exquisite, needle-point spasms of pain. Now I was sure I had whiplash on top of everything else.

While all this was going on, my stud muffin was looking very frustrated that the light was about to change ... and I wasn't even close to making it to the other side of the street. My unsteadiness slowed me. He was yelling at us not too politely, "Hey, ladies, sashay your asses off the goddamn street!" I was creating a situation and this woman's kind assistance was making my faux pas even more obvious to all assembled now on both sides of the street.

The world stopped swirling, replaced by throbbing. But I couldn't turn my head. I wanted to lie down on the asphalt and sleep. As the light changed, we were marooned, abandoned, and firmly fixed in the middle of the busy intersection with people clamoring on all intersection corners. Like frightened, fox-targeted mice, we darted into traffic, dodging and weaving the unforgiving oncoming vehicles. She pulled me along as I still staggered. I felt as if I were on a ledge of a forty-story building, considering jumping. Below my audience was cheering me on to leap or jeering at me for not being speedy enough about doing it to suit them.

By now the exasperated stud muffin had insinuated himself into the fray. Busily directing traffic, he tried to help us make our way across the street. His face grew mean and pinched as unwholesome words flew out of his mouth, "Goddamn stupid women. Don't you dare get hit by a car. I will not have a fatality on my watch. Do you read me loud and clear? Shit!"

Some drivers didn't want to stop for the cop, instead wanting to ooze on through, letting the car behind them stop instead. That caused some verbal altercations between the drivers and my former-Christopher Reeve-wannabe. He was dancing around, slapping the hoods of their vehicles with both hands, and threatening to give them a ticket right then and there.

Once the woman and I had made it safely onto the sidewalk, I glanced back at him and sighed. His face was contorted in a very un-stud muffin-like expression as he shouted at the cars and drivers. I had to chuckle. After my going through all that for him, there was never going to be a smile or a kind word for me from his previously sweet lips. Having now morphed from Superman into Superman's bitter enemy, General Zod, head of the Kryptonian military, he was no longer such a great choice for the object of my affection. After I retrieved my car to return to San Diego, I took side streets in order to avoid his intersection and any further embarrassment or derision.

* *

Resulting Awareness: While physical appearance was always of interest, I was never before interested in more authoritarian or muscular types. My interest in the cop was really an all-time low for me: purely physical. But it was still a sign of my making the choice of whom I'd fancy. Still, I was creating a "Mr. Wrong" in looking to him to respond positively to me.

The question I asked myself: What did I need to do to step back and re-assess attracting and dating so it could possibly be more enjoyable for me.

* * *

Attracting and Dating the Wrong Men?

Massachusetts

It soon felt as if Nature were conspiring against me, indicating I should move back to Massachusetts. First there was my encounter with an impenetrable fog bank that forced me to drive blind for an hour speeding at over-sixty miles per hour to keep up with the heavy traffic flying back from Los Angeles. Next there was an earthquake which shook Scripps Clinic like a rope toy in a dog's mouth. Finally there was a ravaging wildfire in the east which was encroaching on San Diego, reddening the sky and dropping ash and hot embers on us, pock-marking my car's paint job. Before it was contained, San Diego was cordoned off so we spent most of our time lying flat on the floor of our un-air-conditioned apartment, struggling to breathe the dizzying jet-exhaust air. Finally heading east again we rolled over melted and buckled asphalt, surrounded by charred cactus and the bodies of incinerated animals.

Now living in Framingham, I rarely went out on dates, instead spending my time working, studying, and writing. I had tried the singles' bar scene and found it at first inexpressively depressing and then ... just plain boring. There were too many open-polyester-shirted, hairy-chested, "what's you sign?" types physically hanging all over the women, strutting, boasting, and too-obviously "trying to get laid." Rapidly I was becoming discouraged that there were no men with any depth around. They didn't have to be MENSA members but they did have to have two thoughts in their heads they could string together in a sentence that didn't have to do with "how about you and me getting it on, baby."

* * *

19

DOLAN

One cool summer's evening Rosa, my Italian-American friend, and I took advantage of the temperature break to wander around the Boston Common. She had parked her three-year-old black Cadillac off Washington Street, near the Boston Opera House. Walking toward West Street, we turned toward Tremont, passing the Brattle Book Shop. It was one of the oldest and largest used book shops carrying general used books and rare and antiquarian books. I never tired of browsing there. Ever salivating over first editions, I couldn't see them gracing my bookshelves in the near future. We crossed Tremont and considered walking part of the red brick Freedom Trail with its eleven national historical sites representing the American Revolution. But then we decided to cut back toward the Frog Pond. This was where adults and children skated in the winter.

From there we sauntered to Boylston, between Charles Street and Tremont where we found a bar at which singles were hanging out. Sitting at the bar, Rosa had a vodka tonic with a twist of lime while I had cranberry and orange juice with tonic water and a twist. Though tasty, I was sure a shot of vodka could really have gotten it up on its feet. We scanned the room for any sign of a reason to stay longer as we sipped on our possible first round. There were lots of warm bodies: some on the small dance floor gyrating individually, some dancing so intimately they were practically wearing each other's clothing, and others looking comatose or bored in booths or at tables. No one grabbed and held our interest. That is, except the bartender with whom Rosa was flirting. At least she knew it was a terminal exercise despite his interpersonal deftness and expertise. Besides it was too busy to make any real headway with him if that were, indeed, a possibility.

Our drinks finished, we slid off our brown, faux-leather seats and wended our way toward the front entrance. The smoky air and one-hundred-decibel music inside had already given me a headache. As we reached the door, we collided with two nice-looking young men who, likewise having reconnoitered the bar with some dissatisfaction, were leaving. Walking outside together, we exchanged small talk about hot singles' spots in Boston. We decided that most of them were in Cambridge's Kenmore Square, like Lucifer's. They were about my age, possibly a little younger—therefore, considerably younger than Rosa. Chuck, the shorter of the two, who was wearing a pale blue Gap knit shirt, suggested our finding a table at another bar a street over and sharing a quick drink.

The bar he had in mind was mobbed with no tables available. I wasn't interested in doing any more bar hopping, especially after Rosa's and my long walk. So after standing around chatting about trivia for another twenty minutes, Rosa and I casually parted company from our temporary companions. Having nothing else in mind, we decided to head back to Framingham but not before the dark-haired one, who said his name was "Dolan," wanted my phone number to talk some more. But I was reticent. There was something about him that I couldn't pinpoint that bothered me. Rosa impulsively nudged me to give it to him, "Nothing ventured, nothing gained," she whispered, smiling. I eventually did so but with some reluctance.

Forty minutes later, after we located Rosa's car, she had dropped me off at my apartment. No sooner had I walked in the door than the phone rang. It was Dolan. There was an infectious smile in his voice that reminded me of Ken Curtis as Yeoman 3rd Class Dolan in the film version of *Mister Roberts*. The sound suggested that perhaps I was being too hasty in my gut-initiated concern about him. We talked very briefly with him saying he'd like to see me again but, at that particular moment, was just going out for pizza, specifically sausage, anchovies, mushroom, and green-pepper. "I'll touch base with you later." He hung up before I could find out what "later" really meant. It was an odd conversation. Why call me, as he was already heading out the door for a pizza, to tell me he'd call me? Maybe my initial gut feeling about him was what I should listen to.

As I was finishing up in the bathroom, where I had been headed when Dolan called, the phone rang again. Why was Dolan calling again so soon? Or had I left something in Rosa's car? I hurried to answer it. This was before caller-ID. On the line was a serious-sounding, deep-voiced male who claimed to be FBI Agent Barnard Foster. I thought, Come on. This has to be a joke. But in the background were barely distinct official-sounding vocalizations. There was nothing suggesting any levity.

"What do you want? Why are you calling?"

He didn't answer me. Wasting no time, he began to question me. There was specific information he wanted to know. "What's your relationship with the person who just called you?"

"Relationship? There is none."

"How do you know this person then?"

"My friend and I met him and his friend, Chuck, in a bar tonight."

"Where?"

"On Boylston."

"What did you talk about?"

"We thought we might checkout another bar but it also was mobbed. We parted company. They went their way and we went ours. I came home."

"What did he say his name was?"

"He said it was 'Dolan.'"

"Did he give you a last name?"

"No."

"Where does he live?"

"I haven't the foggiest. He didn't say."

"Did he give you his phone number?"

"No."

"What did you talk about on the phone?"

"He said he was going out for pizza."

"He called to say he was going out for pizza?"

"Yes, Sorry. That's what he said."

"Did that have any special meaning for you?"

"No. I have no idea why he bothered to call."

"Did he say where he was going for pizza?"

"No."

"Will he be calling you back?"

"No, I don't expect him to."

"If he does, will you call us?" He gave me a number.

"Yes. But wait a minute. What is this about? Why are you calling me?" The line went dead.

My interrogation lasted about ten minutes until it was obvious to whoever was on the other end of the line that I knew even less than nothing about Dolan, except for his interest in a four-way combo pizza. My chest felt as if an iceberg were resting on it. I was chilled, barely able to breathe. If this was truly the FBI, they must have tapped his phone. How else would they have known to call me? Desperate to know if I had been the brunt of a bad joke, I called the number he gave me. Greeting me was a formal-sounding message on an answering machine that didn't identify it as the FBI's main office.

Did this mean Dolan was under FBI surveillance? Could he have been wanted for questioning in connection with organized or white-collar crime, public corruption, civil rights, or major thefts? I couldn't imagine Dolan being involved in a kidnapping or a series of murders I hadn't heard about. It left me not having any idea about what had happened ... or if there would be repercussions, like my being recorded in someone's file forever as an associate of whoever "Dolan" was.

* *

Resulting Awareness: I had ignored my intuition and let Rosa tell me what to do which I knew was wrong. I was still having difficulties saying, "no" for fear of being negatively evaluated, and so not following what I felt was right for me.

The question I asked myself: What other unconscious allegiances was I following that were interfering with my attracting the "right" men?

* * *

20

JIM

One afternoon in Stop and Shop supermarket I ran into an old friend from high school, Jerry. He had been one-grade behind me and at one point in need of someone to salve his difficulties with being smarter than his fellow students. Now he was a chemical engineer working in Cambridge on a government project. At his lab he had a colleague, Jim, who had recently moved from Virginia to the Cambridge area and wanted to meet women. Jerry told me about him and asked if I'd meet him. He seemed to feel there were the makings of a match between Jim and me. I suspected Jerry wanted to play matchmaker perhaps to repay me. He really shouldn't have.

Jim and I met on the phone and spoke several times before our first in-person meeting over tea at Friendly's Ice Cream in Shoppers World. Everything about him shouted thoughtful, gentle, intelligent, and companionable. He even had a slight, lilting Southern accent. Tall, thin-faced, thirty-something, he looked like the phenotype for a so-called Black Irish male, with dark hair, brown eyes, and a medium skin tone. When we met, he was wearing maroon turtleneck, tan suede jacket, and dark blown slacks which set off his coloring. Quickly I learned he was living in Somerville, just north of Cambridge, was recently divorced, and had an eight-year-old son who lived with his mother in Richmond area. Little did I know the maelstrom I was about to step into.

From the first date on, Saturdays were a problem. This was the day on which he would religiously phone his son. While his regular contact with his son sounded like a thoughtful, loving, fatherly thing to do, it was indelibly etched in basalt that it *had* to be at twelve noon sharp, Saturday-only, no matter what. Since this was before cell phones, it was difficult to do much of anything on this day without this awkward interruption. How Saturdays repeatedly played themselves out soon became a sharp bone of contention sticking in my craw but that was only the appetizer.

That first Saturday he wanted us to meet early because we were going to travel west to check out a miniature horse ranch near Worcester. Jim was already anxious about going out and somehow missing his call in the process.

I suggested, "If you'd prefer, we could wait here and—."

"No," he cut me off.

Annoyed and wanting to finish my thought, "Go out after you call your son. In the meantime, we could relax or do something locally. We could even check out the miniature horses another day."

He looked at me as if I had no right to make this suggestion, especially about his relationship with his son, as well as contradict what he said we would do. Besides, he had already said, "No." Where had I seen that before? He wasn't interested in my trying to make it easier. It was *his* decision ... period ... about *our* time together.

His plan was that we would leave early for our excursion and he would call his son from some place along the way. *Some* place? I silently questioned. That made me uncomfortable. Did he have a particular place in mind from which to call? I could only imagine what that would mean ... and I would have been way off.

Leaving actually took longer than I had expected. There was a constant stream of little things Jim suddenly "needed" to do before we left so we had not yet reached our miniature horse ranch destination as time was drawing nearer to twelve noon. Jim began to search desperately for a telephone. I hadn't seen him looking for phones along the routes we had taken and he hadn't asked me to do it either. Since he had said nothing, I had made the erroneous assumption he already had something in mind. Suddenly we were driving around aimlessly, taking this street then that, doubling back when a cluster of homes magically appeared. For twenty minutes he checked out side roads to find himself a phone.

With a state map from his glove compartment in hand, I was supposed to navigate. But all I could do was inadequately guide him to a more populous area locally, without our having to drive all the way into the city of Worcester. Every direction I gave was questioned or contradicted, adding further to Jim's increasing anxiety and rage. He was talking to himself, ramping up his frustration and fear. It was almost as if he were purposely creating this chaos to undergird the weight of his efforts for his son.

Driving too fast and erratically, sweating, swearing, and tailgating cars in front of him, he muttered through his teeth, "Damn! Things are never where they should be when I need them. I promised I'd call. I have to call. He expects me to call. Son of a bitch, I can't disappoint him."

Unnerved by his dangerously panicky behavior, I didn't know whether I was more afraid of our being in an accident or his having a stroke behind the wheel. By the merest pinch of good fortune's salt tossed over his shoulder, a phone hove into view. It was outside a closed general store in the boondocks, still intact and functional. He was late but he made his connection. For the next half-hour I sat sweltering in the sun-pummeled car in the summer's heat, unsuccessfully surveying the area for any shade to which to escape, as he spoke with his youngster. This scene in its many variations soon played out with regularity.

Despite my attempts to deny what was occurring, in about a month's time I had to acknowledge that everything revolved around Jim. It was what he wanted, when he wanted it, how he wanted it, and where he wanted it. Moreover, he appeared so overwhelmed by guilt as a result of his pain-killer-addicted wife having won a hard-fought battle for custody of their son that he seemed to concentrate all his thoughts, emotions, and energy on his son.

His son came first in any and every conceivable way. It started with my talking to Jim with his son interrupting frequently. Rather than ask his son to wait a moment until we were finished, he immediately responded to his son, leaving me hanging in mid-sentence in person and on the phone for minutes at a time. In addition to the phone calls came the frequent visits by his son. When his son visited, Jim stumbled all over himself to do whatever his son wanted, creating what I considered an unhealthy situation. I was always invited along but I didn't know why since I wasn't even a mote of dust in their presence.

Soon he was letting his son do whatever he wanted, bought him whatever he desired irrespective of price, never scolded or corrected him for errors or bad acts, and never indicated what the appropriate or polite thing to do was. When the boy threw a large rock at a nearby cat, fortunately barely missing it, I went ballistic. But Jim did nothing about it. Moreover, he was very angry with me for taking his son to task. That created a large rift between us.

Becoming an all-powerful, dictatorial little emperor, his son had picked up on these behavioral dynamics quickly. He was learning how to get whatever he wanted whenever he wanted it. He tended to steer clear of trying to work his charms on me, however, because I was on the sidelines watching the action, immune. With his father's unconscious permission, he toyed with his dad's enormous gunny sack full of guilt to not only gain attention but also punish his dad for his perceived abandonment.

In a moment of unexpected self-revelation, his son shared with me his hatred for his father for having betrayed and left him and his mother. Jim couldn't see anything beyond his own attempts at atonement for his sin of not having won his case in court. How he realistically would have been able to take care of his son if he had won the case was beside the point. Winning was, however, all-important. This was a time when the mother almost always won custody, unless there were dire negative circumstances on her part which couldn't be masked by her family.

Shackled to his child, Jim couldn't see the outward behavioral expressions of his uncontrolled son. Consequently, his son commanded his being flown to Somerville and back to Richmond with a snap of his fingers. With his being blind to the situation, Jim was constantly being sucked into his son's every ploy to the inexcusable detriment of his son. Sadly his son did grow into an irresponsible, self-absorbed adult who expected his father to rescue him from any problem, which his father always did, but who still hated his father.

While initially seeming quite attractive and charming as we began dating, Jim slowly revealed another side of himself. Always making jokes, he thought of himself as having a great sense of humor. However, it was sarcasm that he held to be the highest form of sophisticated humor. He never saw its hostility, aggression, and derisiveness which he all too frequently aimed at me. He often made fun of whatever I said and put down my ideas, feelings, actions, and work. He'd laugh and I'd retort, "I didn't find that funny. It hurt." My response gave him the occasion to dramatically roll his eyes as if to say, "You have no sense of humor" or to indicate that he thought I lacked the intellect to understand and appreciate his wit. It also gave him the opportunity to argue that, in essence, I was stupid for feeling that way, that I didn't have the *right* to feel hurt. He loved to argue ... about anything, no matter how trivial.

Bit by little bit his behaviors illuminated a strongly controlling and manipulative personality, the same behaviors he was unknowingly teaching his son. In many ways he was like my father's twin. That increasing awareness frightened me more because he was not the first man I had had an acquaintance with who mirrored my father.

Jim's most outstanding characteristic was that he had to be right ... all the time, smarter than anyone else, and the winner of any perceived competition. If a competition didn't exist, he'd create one. Typically his M.O. was to tell me I was wrong then drown me in a river of ludicrous reasons that I was wrong or a series of absurd predictions resulting from my position. Each would be more far-fetched than the last in order to support his contention. His objective seemed to be correcting me, having the final word on some subject, as well as trying to push me into agreeing with his original take on some issue.

One evening I was cooking paella. Having sautéed the sausage and chicken, I had removed them from the pan and sautéed the onions, garlic, and parsley then added the tomatoes, letting the mixture caramelize a touch. Folding in the uncooked rice and chicken stock, I covered it and was going to let it simmer for ten minutes to make the rice tender before adding the shrimp. Nature was calling so I checked the flame and raced to the bathroom. When I returned moments later, Jim was pacing back and forth in front of the stove, hrumphing.

When he saw me, he accused, "You left this cooking unattended. Do you know how dangerous that is? The rice could have dried out, making the pan white hot, setting the counter on fire. Flames could have crawled up the wall into the overhead cabinets and started the kitchen ablaze. Getting out of the apartment would have been nearly impossible in the smoke and flame a kitchen fire can cause. There would have been no way we could have put out the fire. The fire department couldn't have gotten here in time. We could have been killed."

I responded, "The pan was on simmer and I was gone for only a moment." I knew better than to say anything further.

"But it only takes a moment to create a fiery holocaust and then it's too late to consider turning off the flame before you leave. Do you know how many fires start in the kitchen? The statistics are astounding."

When confronted with this flood of worst-case scenarios, there was little point in my saying more. Simply repeating myself to him made no sense. I wasn't going to out-argue or outlast him. And in Jim's case, it made even less sense because he would never acknowledge that my opinions or knowledge could possibly have any validity or weight.

Irrespective of what we were discussing—from the defoliant Agent Orange to lasagne condiments to the weather—he would take an adversarial position, telling me why what I said was wrong or it couldn't be true. This was even if it ultimately turned out he agreed with my original premise or position, but, of course, he never acknowledged it.

Interestingly, whenever I said something with which he could argue, he revealed a poker player's *tell*—a small nonverbal behavior he did unconsciously in every one of these situations. It was a supercilious smile puckering his lips accompanied by a small all-knowing chuckle. Without having to shake his head and laugh aloud at what he considered to be my obvious deficiency, he was readying himself to contradict, correct me, and argue for as long as it took to make himself feel he had accomplished his goal, triumphant. It was as if he had to put me down to raise himself up. I came to loathe that simpering smirk, wanting to wipe it off his face in whatever way I could.

It could not have been more self-evident than if that terrorist pigeon had returned to plotz on my head once again. This narcissism-plagued situation was in every way on a downward spiral of mutually-assured-destruction. This was evolving into the grand opera of psychodramas and I didn't want to be any part of it then or in the future.

* *

Resulting Awareness: Because Jim was so like my father I fell back into the old relationship behaviors I had with my father. I unconsciously allowed myself to become a victim and tolerated how Jim thoughtlessly and cruelly treated and manipulated me for longer than I should have. Slowly, however, I saw what I was doing and why and asserted myself. The familiar is always seductive irrespective of how painful it is. It's like "the devil you know is better than the devil you don't know."

The question I asked myself: How important was it for me to be in familiar patterns that hurt me than in new, less familiar patterns that were more positive even if a little scary?

* * *

Attracting and Dating the Wrong Men?

After that, I didn't go out for what seemed like eons, but it was only a little more than a year. As a last resort but with a lot of trepidation, I contemplated computer dating. Before Internet dating, this required me to fill out a long paper questionnaire. The information from it was then typed onto punch cards to be read by a machine. It resulted in my receiving a dot-matrix-print-out by post of those with whom I was "matched," along some unknown, seemingly inexplicable dimensions. Each name carried with it a few words of description and their phone numbers. The men were expected to call the women.

However, it soon became all too clear that computer daters' descriptions of themselves were often bordering on Fantasyland. That is not to say that they lied ... exactly ... about their age, interests, marital status, parental status, appearance, profession, or dating goals. They were, charitably-speaking, simply being overly kind to themselves. Research has indicated that as many as ninety percent of those participating in any kind of computer dating are consciously deceptive in their descriptions.

Irrespective of what they claimed, they were not your athletic, outgoing, vivacious types with an IQ above 100, curious about the world, reading more than the sports page, and possessing a fun sense of humor—what I was seeking in some form. Instead, they were avoirdupois, balding, and harried couch potato parents who had memorized NFL stats. They yearned to have their Sundays unfettered and free again to watch their favorite football teams slug it out over Doritos chips, chugalugging their chilled Budweisers. They no longer wanted to have to worry about the laundry, vacuuming, or getting a meal on the table for the kids. The majority of the men I ended up being "matched" with were middle-aged daddies who were desperate to find a live-in nanny-housekeeper, maybe a wife, but not necessarily someone for an intellectually-, emotionally-, or athletically stimulating, meaningful, or fun relationship. I had little faith in the computer-dating's so-called "matching."

* * *

21

DR. HARVARD

One of my first computer dates was a physician from Harvard Medical School. I had high hopes for this one since I was still medically-oriented and kept up-to-date with the *Journal of the American Medical Association* and the *New England Journal of Medicine*. But by now my chances of going to medical school seemed to be approaching zero. Arranging the date by phone, we met at a pub off Washington Street in Newton. The ambiance was casual and reminiscent of homey English pubs with dark wood wainscoting, pendant lights with large globes, dark booths, and a long mirrored bar with stools. No televisions or blaring jukeboxes spoiled the relaxed atmosphere.

He arrived shortly after I did. Very tall, perhaps six-five to my five-three, he sported light red wavy hair, cut but somewhat wild-looking, and a pink face. Today he could have been a sibling of Conan O'Brien. What was startlingly noticeable from the moment he appeared was that he hardly ever looked at me. It was very disconcerting. I felt as if I had missed my lips with my lipstick decorating my cheek or had put my pantyhose on over my head. Perhaps what I really needed was to be dressed in a hospital johnny or surgical gown for him to actually look at me.

Once we were seated at a table, he ordered British cheese on toast, London broil, a salad of arugula and roasted peppers, and a Guinness. I had fish and chips with a blue cheese and bacon coating, coleslaw, and hot Earl Grey tea. Throughout the one-hour meal, he talked endlessly about himself. Consequently, I learned all sorts of quasi-personal things about what he did, and by implication, what he didn't do. Mostly I learned about surgical techniques, how to separate individual organs from spouting arteries during surgery, and the pathology research he had done—both excellent dinner topics if you had a strong stomach. As he spoke, ostensibly to me, he eyes remained closed. The only time he opened them was to spear another hunk of beef.

My attempted contributions about medicine or myself were not commented upon. Instead he proceeded to describe a new surgical instrument he was inventing. It was something for removing your appendix—maybe through your rectum, or was it through your nose? There were too many inconsequential details to remember. As we had dessert, he had a scone with clotted cream and I had a jaffa cake, a small piece of cake filled with orange jam and covered with chocolate, I started playing a guessing game with myself about his eyes. Did he think he had been allotted only so many blinks and didn't want to waste them? Did he think that by not using his sight socially he was saving it for work? Finishing his meal, he raised his head with eyes closed, unenthusiastically thanked me and left the pub.

Following behind, I conjectured that his anxiety was worse than mine about this blind date. Perhaps he was more likely to have had an engaging interaction with an anesthetized body on an operating table or a slime mold on a glass slide under a microscope. Or, perhaps, he thought I'd be so honored by his sharing his illustrious presence with me that his paying attention to me was unnecessary. Irrespective of whatever it might have been, I had to feel sorry for any individual who would have to talk with him in his professional capacity as a "doctor."

Attracting and Dating the Wrong Men?

* *

Resulting Awareness: I had idolized medicine, therefore, anyone connected with it represented the end-all and be-all. This encounter plus my other experiences with men in the medical field had finally made me realize that there was nothing all that special about them. They could be "wrong men" as easily as anyone else. What was more important than what they did was how their interests melded with mine. That suggested I would have to join groups which represented my interests to find more likely companions.

The question I asked myself: What behavioral and attitudinal criteria, not job or profession, did I really want to match in someone I would want to date?

* * *

22

HARVEY

After a few more "illustrious" dates over several more months, I was ready to put a finger down my throat and call computer dating, or any kind of dating for that matter, quits. Just then I received a call from a dentist named Harvey who was way down on my several-page printout. Located in a nearby town, he sounded intelligent, like a professional person, but with other interests, such as art and architecture. He appeared to have potential in that he didn't sound clingy, desperate, or totally disengaged. So we talked briefly by phone for a while before we decided to meet. My in-person-meeting rule now was that it would have to be in a *public* place on *neutral ground* at a location *I knew* where I had *my own car* with me.

"Let's make it for a late lunch at the café near my newly-re-furbished dental practice," he suggested. "I have an early day on Thursday. I want you to see what I've had done. The office looks so modern. You know, crisp, and clean ... glass and chrome. It was a very good investment."

There was no question from the level of enthusiasm he exuded over the phone that he was dying to show off his "new professional office." The lunch part sounded okay because it would be in a restaurant though not exactly on neutral territory and definitely not some place I knew, never having been to his town. Seeing his office was questionable at this point. This was not a good sign. Already I was contemplating contradicting two of my rules.

Finally I relented. I informed him I would meet him at the café and follow him to his office. At least I would have my car with me in case things didn't go well. Knowing I could leave at any time was necessary to my feeling more in control. He gave me directions and I checked a map. He was far out, to the west and beyond Route 495, but I felt confident this would not be a problem even though I could not actually locate the streets on my folding area map. Unfortunately, Google maps did not exist at this time so I was winging it in my approximations. Despite my generally very good navigational skills, I found myself lost on the way there once I left 495.

Everything suddenly felt foreign to me, as if I were the middle of nowhere, like an alien planet, where nothing was where it should be. Houses, cars, traffic, road signs, and signs of life were non-existent. It felt as if they had not yet been placed in this model train's scenic landscape. My internal compass seemed not to be working. It was highly unusual for me to be lost ... but I was well and truly lost.

As I kept driving, I finally spotted a call box along the side of the road. I called him, "Harvey, I'm just about ten miles off Rt. 495 and I'm lost. There are no road signs or markers out here. Can you come guide me to the café from here? I'm in a green VW Rabbit, sitting on the side of the road."

He agreed to meet me but thought my following him to the café was ill-advised. He explained, "There are no streetlights out here so you may have difficulty finding your way back after dark. Perhaps it would be better if I picked you up. Then I can drop you back off at your car later."

My blood pressure rose. The hair at the back of my neck stood straight up. Leaving my car behind did not appeal to me. But I found I could make neither hide nor hair of where I was. For a moment I wondered if he had given me the right directions to the café. Did he have a problem with sense of direction? Or I had misheard or misinterpreted them? This was the depth of the hinterlands, isolated, intimidating, and displeasing for a female alone as the afternoon was cashing in.

A voice in the back of my head was telling me to turn around and go home. I really needed to re-schedule the lunch date for some place I knew, but it felt so awkward. And once again I worried he might reject me as a result. My father had rejected me for being a girl when he wanted a boy. I didn't want to be reminded how that felt. Most reluctantly I agreed to ride with him to the luncheonette, leaving my car on the side of the road. Concerned my car would be ticketed as abandoned and, perhaps, even towed away, I let Harvey assuage my fears to a degree. "This road isn't patrolled all that frequently so I wouldn't worry about getting a ticket."

From what I had seen so far, I could attest to the lack of a police presence. If only a cop had come by, I could have been directed to the café in no time flat. Moreover, I would not have to be hitching a ride with Harvey. Bit by little bit I was giving up my control and my safety, potentially putting myself at risk. When he arrived to pick me up in his burgundy Mercedes-Benz, I was still filled with conflict. Then I saw Harvey for the first time. My conflict intensified.

Not having seen a picture of Harvey beforehand, I didn't know what to expect. He was swarthy, perhaps Middle Eastern or North African, short, squat, and beefy. It was only then I recognized that his last name could be seen as perhaps "Persian" or "Algerian," or something in that region of the world. While it appeared from our conversations he had been born in this country, his possible cultural background now concerned me. I didn't want to stereotype him and make unjust assumptions but Middle Eastern and North African countries were often patriarchal and frequently governed by very conservative, strict religious dictates. Sadly they were not known for valuing their women, treating them well, much less respecting them as equals. Hopefully if this was his male-dominated heritage, it would not be a something he expressed in his behavior. I consoled myself it was only lunch ... and just this one.

Emotionally shaking my head, I sucked in my concerns and left with him in his "Mister Benz." After my earlier less-than-pleasant dating experiences, I tended to reside on the periphery of paranoia, or, perhaps, it was hyper-vigilance and super-caution, yet I went with him anyway. "Mister Benz" followed the twists and turns of the road, hugging the asphalt and tracking flawlessly as well it should have being one of the three best-selling luxury cars in the world and, at the time, known for its precise German engineering.

Upon finally reaching Harvey's small town's main thoroughfare, I recognized that I would not have found it easily by his directions or the route we took. As we cruised along at twenty-five miles per hour, I saw a little town that had seen better days, sorely in need of revitalization. I also noticed on the left side of the main drag we had just rolled past a café calling attention to itself by its overhung green-and-white-striped awning. Was that our destination? Our car continued to travel. It was soon apparent we had bypassed the only eating establishment in town. Now we were winding around back roads that had woven themselves through a forest, ones that I assumed would ultimately lead us to his sparkling, antiseptic-looking office. It was a conundrum how any medical business could survive buried in this arboreal denseness so far from town. I couldn't imagine his clients following this circuitous path for their appointments.

My paranoia was roiling under the surface with ever-larger bubbles rising and popping. Was this the most direct route or the maze-like "scenic" route he wanted to show off? His having ignored the restaurant and traveled through stands of timber to get to his office was twitching my antennae, signaling distress.

We stopped in front of a white, two-story, wood-framed house with his shingle out front. The first floor had a bump out in front which projected well beyond the second floor like a bulldog's under-slung jaw to give his downstairs office more space. As we were about to get out of his car, I turned to him said, "Harvey, it's getting late and I'm really quite hungry. I thought we were going to have lunch first." He didn't respond but opened his door and got out. Over the shiny hood of his car, I said, "If you don't mind, I'd like to make this office tour brief so we can get back to doing what we had planned." My rising anxiety was making me sound food-obsessed but I didn't care.

He still didn't respond. I couldn't discern if he hadn't heard me or if he were ignoring me. From the expression forming on his face his mind was likely on ceremoniously unveiling his pride and joy, his newly renovated office. This was to be the grand tour to end all grand tours. Arms wide, stepping over the threshold, he presented the waiting room to me as if he were a couturier and this were his new fall fashion line.

To the right of the front door was a large waiting room with comfortable-looking brown leather and chrome chairs, chrome-legged glass topped tables with a variety of reading material. Surrounded by different types of dracaena, philodendron, ficus, and palms in large pots on the floor, it whispered a green tranquility and relaxation. To the left was his circular glass-block reception desk welcoming patients to enter. The area was less minimalist than I had imagined. His eagerness was tangible. Confidentially disclosing how much he had paid for the work, he wanted me to appreciate every structural, mechanical, and aesthetic detail that had gone into creating this contemporary state-of-of-the-art dental masterpiece, sure to be a cover feature in *Architectural Digest*.

While there was still more to see, I wanted to leave. He escorted me past he reception desk to his four small treatment rooms each with its own dental chair: examination, hygienist, orthodontic, and surgical. This allowed him to accommodate all his clients whether they were there for cleaning, new crowns, straightening, or some invasive procedure. In each treatment room, he extolled its individual virtues in the minutest detail. I didn't really want to know about the x-ray machines, scalers, the three kinds of probes: sickle, periodontal, and straight; or retractors: cheek, tongue, and lip. And I most assuredly didn't want to know about the different types of excavators he had and employed.

There was also a tiny lab where he could match crown colors and make alginate for taking impressions, and a unisex restroom which was also accessible from the back of the waiting room. Everywhere the walls were hung with attractive prints by well-known artists and original oils of landscapes, all with expensive frames. My small plastic smile, while now drooping at the corners, was still in place as I continued to mutter all the appropriate words of recognition. Adding to my increasing discomfort, my stomach was growling audibly and demanding of me to get it some sustenance. The afternoon was fast disappearing.

After he finished his attention-numbing promotional spiel, he invited me upstairs to see his apartment above his practice. "I decided to renovate this as well. You'll be amazed at its elegance and beauty."

"Thanks but I'm already overwhelmed. Another time, perhaps. I think we ought to go have that lunch." I suggested pleasantly, trying to get us back on track for this so-called "date." My wishes, so far, had been disregarded.

"Wait. We'll get to it," he answered then started to ascend the dark staircase which was centered in the entryway and in direct line with the front door. There were luxuriant potted plants on the lower staircase steps to discourage patients from ascending.

I thought, "Come on, Harvey. I have no desire to shuffle through another interior design tour. I like Bauhaus architecture but enough already. I want to eat lunch as promised ... and go home." Minute by minute my dislike for this situation was growing. I'd been to enough men's apartments to know that no matter what they claimed, this was where their secretive plans of seduction were being hatched. Once again I didn't feel in control of the situation but hadn't as yet figured out what to do.

As someone who had left her car on some hitherto unnamed satellite of Earth, I knew I didn't have much choice. "Okay," I told myself, "I can calmly and pleasantly see the rest of it. I can be a good guest. Maybe he hasn't had much chance to show off his refurbishment. He's understandably excited about what he's done. Give him a little more slack. I'll do the next tour and then we'll go have lunch. I need to put myself in a less stressful frame of mind."

Having begun to hyperventilate, breathing fast and shallowly from my upper lungs, I was breathing out too much carbon dioxide. Dizziness was only breaths away if I didn't re-balance my oxygen and carbon dioxide levels. Visualizing myself soaking in a warm, aromatic tub, surrounded by lighted candles and strains of Debussy wafting on a cool breeze, I regained some composure. Following him up the stairs, my gut was reminding me, "Be careful not to let him see you are anxious or afraid."

When he flipped the 150-watt overhead light at the top to illuminate the stairwell, I inhaled loudly in surprise. What greeted me was a keyhole-shaped opening in which his apartment door was set. Above it were large swaths of reddish-brown paint following its curvature on the walls. The door itself was a dark-stained cedar Moroccan lattice screen. But this was nothing compared to what smacked me in the face when he unlocked and opened the door.

"Oh my!" I exclaimed involuntarily as I was taken aback by the unexpected.

"I knew you'd like it."

Before me was a recreation of an early Hollywood set of something from the Arabian Nights. I half anticipated a 1930's Douglas Fairbanks, dashing, young, athletic, bare-chested, and smiling, to swing in on a golden rope from a nearby balcony. The four windows were draped in a floor-length, red diaphanous material, secured at the sides by large ornate brass holdbacks.

From the roughly-plastered white ceiling hung four large six-sided glass and punctured brass lanterns on long chains. Complex-designed, multicolored tiles formed twenty-by-twenty-inch squares and diamond-shapes embedded in the walls. On the floor was what looked like a nine-by-twelve Tabriz Persian rug in dark blue with an intricate diamond-shaped floral center, surrounded by filigree in deep gold and red, and different colored bands running around the outer perimeter. On it was a carved dark cedar coffee table, inlaid with mother of pearl. Its inward-curved legs seemed to buckle like a tired donkey trying to lie down. These two dramatic items made his long, cordovan Naugahyde sofa against the wall stand out in eccentric relief.

"Words fail me," I commented, not fully at one with the scenic designer's décor concept. "You certainly seem to have captured an artistic Moorish room."

He led me around the twenty-by-fifteen room from wall to wall and nook to niche, pointing out a heavily decorated large, red buffet with four drawers on top and three painted panel doors which he said came from Marrakesh. There was also a very ornate three-by-five-foot vertical silver mirror of camel bone inlaid with cedar wood. This "Shama mirror" was, he said, "one of a kind" as were some of the large, hand tooled-with-metal "Touareg pottery urns" which sat on the floor. Smaller pieces of antique-looking pottery were everywhere along with his collection of Saudi Arabian, North African, and Bedouin coffee servers tin-plated or made of brass with their flip-hinged lids and long, hollow handles. He described the cultural history of each piece and how he had acquired it. Sensory overload was deadening my brain cells.

As I scrutinized all the intricate, filigree-like work or hand-etched geometric folk art motifs, his mood changed. He grabbed my arms, quickly turning me around to face him. He was already puckered, ready to kiss me.

"Harvey, wait," I said, trying to recapture the previous mood. "Let's slow down a little. How about a little chat? We haven't had a chance for one yet." It felt imperative that I try to get him to take his foot off the gas as soon as possible. Talking, making suggestions, and asking questions held promise. "And what about our having that nice leisurely lunch you promised? You must be a little hungry. I know I am. Can you make lunch here? Maybe sandwiches and something to drink, iced tea, perhaps? I could give you a hand. You know, you haven't told me about how you decided to become a dentist. I'd really like to hear about it."

But once again he didn't react. He didn't follow through with his pucker either. It was as if he had gone someplace else, into another dimension. Looking as if he were momentarily hypnotized, he led me, his hand still clutching my upper arm, to his nine-foot-long sofa. Perhaps, I thought, he wants to sit here to talk, to get to know each other here, rather than over a meal. I didn't like it because eating a meal would have provided some distraction and promoted less intimacy.

He seemed to be responding to half of my request. If we talked awhile, it might get me out of there sooner. While I was trying to make the best of the lemons I had been handed, I didn't see any lemonade being squeezed out of them. But, then again, I wasn't about to run out this apartment door, down the stairs, through his dental office, and to his car for which I didn't have keys. Besides I had no idea where the town or main road was.

As I started to sit, he quickly shifted his weight. He threw me down. I landed on my back on his over-stuffed faux-leather sofa. In a flash he was on top of me, puckering again. But this was not going to be a romantic Arabian Nights' movie, like *Ali Baba and the Forty Thieves* with exotically handsome Turhan Bey. It was going to be anything but. I couldn't catch my breath. "I can't breathe," I wheezed. He didn't respond, still trying to reach my lips. So I proposed an exchange. "Harvey," I gulped, "if I let you kiss me, will you get off me? I really can't breathe."

But my attempt at getting a quid pro quo was not having the desired effect. Apparently he and I were working from very different scripts. He was Charles Bronson in *Death Wish* while I was Shirley Temple in *Rebecca of Sunnybrook Farm*. He kissed me, not playfully. He was rapidly becoming more aggressive. This was turning into a wrestling match where my Revlon-rouged lips were no longer the goal. Everything I'd done to this point, however innocently ... or stupidly, had helped create a real problem. My being pleasant and interested in interior design was apparently a turn on for him. But, then again, if I had been rude or unappreciative, that might have created an even worse scenario. The risk of sexual assault was imminent if I didn't think of something ... quickly.

What could I do with my spine glued to the fabric-backed polyvinyl cushions? I didn't have any leverage with my legs and my arms were already pinned to my sides. I had a skirt on and didn't want to reveal too much leg in the process which might only further encourage him. With his assumed North African or Middle Eastern background I worried he would likely try to acquire what he wanted from me irrespective. He was already sweating, panting, groping, without the need of any male enhancement. Overpowering him, sending his corpulent body tumbling onto the floor, was out of the question given my current position.

The only strength I could think to employ was my ability to talk calmly and rationally in a crisis. "Harvey," I began with a firm but breath-impaired tone, "What you are attempting to do will not accomplish what you want." I reasoned with him, "What you ultimately want to achieve—our being close—is out of the question if you pursue it this way. This is not the proper course of action for you or me." I droned on and on, grabbing air where I could. I didn't think I could change his mind but maybe I could bore him into a little sensibility, assuming he was listening. In his testosterone-bathed state, I could become a statistic in the crime news in the local paper.

I continued with my monologue, "If you like me and want me to like you, you are going about it in the wrong way. I have to respect you to like you. You want me to respect you, don't you? But if you continue as you are, I won't be able to." After twenty minutes of listening to my soporific blah-blah-blah lecture, he rose robotically to a sitting position again.

As I blessedly filled my lungs with oxygen, I noted something was different. It wasn't as though he had simply changed his mind and wanted to approach our "possible relationship" in a different way. His body language was off. It was as if he'd turned a page in a book he was reading and was on a new chapter. He had entered that parallel universe again. Suddenly, attempts at kissing me were all behind him. Rape, or his version of "making love," was likewise. It was as if it had never occurred. Now, suddenly, he was enthusiastically sharing his future plans for us.

"You'll like our future." Grinning like a child with its first bicycle, he was ecstatic. "Tomorrow morning you and I will gather all our necessary gear, clothing, and food. Then we'll saddle up 'Sexy Sarah.'" Pausing only to explain that "Sexy Sarah" was his beloved Harley, he continued. "We'll start for Colorado." We were to be easy riders embarking on an open-road trip to fulfill our destiny ... together.

"We'll set up housekeeping in a log cabin the Rocky Mountains, near Estes Park. We'll raise chickens. We can stay there indefinitely." He was nearly laughing with glee, his eyes dreamily on the prize he was envisioning. I was silent for a moment, letting him bask in the sheer delight he had created for himself as I considered my options.

He seemed to have totally forgotten his up-dated dental practice and remitted his newly created Moroccan seraglio to the past. I knew I had to carefully acknowledge his dream but step away from it. I didn't dare say I'd go with him tomorrow to placate him for fear he might decide to take me up on it then and there. That could have been worse. I was hoping a little reality could seep through to change his plan. "That does sound like an exciting adventure. I'm sure you will enjoy it immensely. But," I tried to include a note of regret in my voice, "I'm not available to go. I have undergraduate courses to teach. There is no way I can leave with the heavy schedule I have at Framingham State College. Besides I'm allergic to chickens."

Suddenly he blinked. As his smile vanished, his body language changed again. It was so slight but so dramatic that it could almost have been a petit mal seizure. I was afraid to say another word. The situation felt dangerous. He looked broodingly angry, like an actor trying on different hostile expressions in a mirror. A twinge of fear cinched my gut. Something was going on. I wasn't sure what but knew I would have to do something about it. The brain-numbing drone I had used earlier might not work a second time.

Scanning the area, I looked around for anything I could use as a cudgel in case. There was nothing. The large pots were too unwieldy to lift and the small pots and coffee servers were inadequate to the task. Where was the phone up here? I hadn't noticed one in my tour of the living room. If I could find one and call 911 or a cab, I could tell them I was at his office and come get me. But I didn't see one. He must have a phone up here. I knew he had one downstairs. Perhaps I could slip down there to use it.

He rose from the sofa with determination. Without a word he revealed his keys and locked the front and back doors. The backdoor opened onto a steep white-painted staircase that came to rest in his grassed backyard. Moving about stealthily, he located three seemingly camouflaged phones that had been stationed around his large living room, kitchen, and bedroom and unplugged them one by one. Cradling them to his chest, he walked slowly into his non-Moorish-style bedroom off the living room to the right. As if in a fugue, there he crawled onto his bed, facing the living room. On the dark blue bedspread he assumed a fetal position. In very little time he was asleep, still clutching the phones to him.

I began analyzing the situation aloud, "I don't have access to a phone up here to call the police or a cab or anyone or anything else. So how can I get out of his apartment? To get downstairs to his office I would have to lift his keys. I didn't see him put his keys down any place so they must be in his pants pocket. But trying to lift them, I would be risking awakening him. If that happened, I have no idea what mood he would be in then. But it would be worth a try unless I can think of something better to do."

I tiptoed into his bedroom. In his fetal position one pants pocket was under him, unavailable, but the other was above. Curled onto himself, he had created a slight pocket opening at the top. The bottom of it, however, was caught in the crease of the fabric folds at his meaty groin. I walked behind the bed, approaching him from the rear.

Ever-so-slowly, I gently fingered the pocket gap. He moved, curling more tightly. I held my breath. My middle finger slid a fraction of an inch into his pocket but found nothing ... as far as it went. In case the keys might be deeper, I let my middle finger sink another eighth of an inch. Nothing. At the same time he snorted. My heart stopped. "Don't let me die here" I begged whatever gods might be listening and in charge of cardiac arrest deaths.

The keys had to be in his other pocket. It was then I remembered Harvey using his left hand when he unlocked and locked the doors. That meant he probably kept his keys in his left-hand pocket, the one on which he was lying. There was no way I was getting his keys unless he turned over on his other side. I would just have to keep watch. Monitoring his breathing as I moved cautiously back around the bed, I tiptoed out to the living room.

I wanted out. I wanted out ... now! It seemed there was nothing I could do but wait. I didn't want to wait. Running through my possible options, I started muttering to myself again. Thinking aloud, hearing my own voice and my own thoughts, helped keep me centered and made the thoughts easier to weigh. "First, without a key, I'd have to pick the lock to get downstairs to his office. I don't know how to pick a lock. Besides I'd need thin tools, something to act as a pick and something to act as a tension bar, which I don't have anyway. In lieu of picking the lock, I could try to take the door off its hinges by loosening the pins." I knew from experience that would make a lot of noise and awaken Harvey. If I could, however, that would offer the simplest, most straightforward solution.

Another thought came to mind. "What if I could climb out a window, clamber across the roof, and shin down a drain pipe or jump the twenty feet to the ground if necessary. What would that do for me, assuming I didn't injure myself in the process?" I looked out the windows. The two picture windows facing front which were over the bump out didn't open. The two windows on the sides of the house were situated under the peaks of the sharply-pointed roof. Irrespective of their placement relative to the roofline, they were nailed shut, as was the window in the kitchen.

"Okay, let's assume I actually somehow could get outside, then what? Try to steal his car? His car would have to be unlocked because I don't carry a slim jim or a wire coat hanger with me. Then I'd have to know how to hotwire the car without electrocuting myself. However, I still have no idea where I am and how to get back to town and the main drag. And the risk of getting stuck outside until he wakes up with nothing to show for it sounds really stupid. I'm not about to try to hiking through the woods ... even if I had a compass."

Pain was engulfing me. I was developing a tension headache. The muscles in my shoulders were contracting the muscles in my neck. The muscle sheaf around my skull was acting like a giant vice. Dehydration was also setting in since I had had nothing to drink since before I had left my house in the afternoon. And my stomach was feeling sickeningly hollow. "All right," I bitterly saluted myself, "I've looked at the options and weighed them. Now, apparently all I can do is to wait him out." Seated in a chair that gave me a clear view through the open door of his bedroom, I worked to remain wide-eyed as the hours continued to snail their way along into the night. It was now dark outside.

As I finished my anxiety-ridden calculations, I recognized the telltale signs that indicated my bladder was reaching its critical strain-gauge peak. Holding my Kegel muscles against the urgent pressure, I walked with my thighs together to the bathroom to the left off the living room. The door had no lock. I shivered, contemplating being trapped in the bathroom with my underpants down around my ankles, but I had to go ... now! It came down to my chancing that I'd probably be safe from intruders or soaking myself in urine, like Hebrides-produced tweed cloth. Get real, I thought. I was not about to sit in smelly sogginess for the next ten or so hours.

Assuming the stance, I stretched my hand toward the bathroom door as a precaution, as if it truly could help should someone wish to enter. Entreating my bladder to cooperate and do so as quickly as possible, I straddled the toilet awkwardly. Despite all that rigid muscle tension, my urinary sphincter released itself. The relief was long and absolute, a smattering of heaven in my current hell. When I cautiously opened the bathroom door, ironically I breathed a deep sigh of relief that he was still asleep where I'd left him. But, alas, he had not turned over.

Morning light came grudgingly, the night fighting with its last breath to hold onto its inkiness. I was exhausted and felt sweaty and grubby from still being in yesterday's wrestling-match togs. My teeth were as fuzzy as my tongue. I didn't dare breathe into my cupped hand to see how bad my breath was for fear of strangling myself.

Harvey arose around eight o'clock, leaving the phones in a pile on the bed. He greeted me smiling. He was acting as if he had just returned from a relaxing two-week Cancun vacation by the pool with a Margarita in hand and a couple of "hot bikinied babes" at his bidding.

"Let's go to breakfast." he said brightly. I waited with bated breath for mention of Sexy Sarah ... the Rockies ... or chickens. I was still holding my breath as he unlocked his apartment front door that things might rapidly, unexpectedly reverse themselves.

"Good idea," I replied. Once we were outside, I made a point of looking at my watch, "It's getting late. I have to get back for my late morning class." I added with as big a smile as I could manage under the circumstances, "So we need to hurry."

He unlocked his car door and released the passenger side. Out of curiosity I glanced at the drainpipe which was attached to the side of the house and the gutters. It was only loosely bolted and would have sent me tumbling to the ground if I had clung to it to shinny down. Moreover, if I could have gotten onto the bump out, the wide boxwood hedge that hugged the house's foundation had unyielding trimmed branches which would have made my jumping and landing safely difficult. I was at once glad I had been unable to try to execute my *Mission: Impossible* roof-crawling caper, irrespective of anything else.

This time we drove directly to the main drag, which was, not surprisingly, a short distance away and pulled up in front of the café instead of bypassing it again. If he had taken me back to my car without breakfast, I would not have minded one iota but it seemed judicious not to suggest it. The café's green and white awning above the storefront was fraying significantly, reflecting how I felt. Inside it smelled of grease and weeks of re-circulated cigarette smoke. We sat in front by the large, hand-smudged plate glass window.

He ordered a hearty meal of three eggs, bacon, sausage, fried potatoes, muffin, and coffee, savoring every little morsel. He ate as if he hadn't eaten in days. In between bites, he told me, "I had a really great time on our first date. I look forward to our next." I managed a small smile. He stuffed half a buttered corn muffin into his mouth which caused him to begin to choke. But several quick gulps of coffee softened and dislodged it. "Better luck next time," I thought.

Smiling blandly at his monologue about how pleased he was we had met, I sipped my herbal tea, which was all I'd ordered. He hadn't even noticed. All the while, I kept an eye out for a slowly passing police car in case I needed it. I thought I could tell them my car had stalled and ask for a ride back. No one was going to believe their local dentist had wigged out, kidnapped, and nearly raped me. Nothing appeared as I continued to scan both ends of the street. Managing to stay reasonably calm, I tried to get him to hurry up. I wanted to get going ... before he changed his mind ... again. This time he might whisk me off to Colorado, perhaps in a nitrous oxide-induced state of unconsciousness, lashed to the back of Sexy Sarah.

As if all were right with his world, he finished, chatted with his waitress, telling Betty she should see his new dental suite, and left a paltry tip. Then he escorted me back to his car. On the alert, I was afraid he might turn around and head back to his office so I made a point of not securing my seatbelt. I was prepared to throw open the door and leap out into the street if necessary. Making a scene and injuring myself would have been the least of my concerns at that point.

But the Fates were with me. He drove me back to my awaiting vehicle. The windshield boasted no ticket under the wiper. He had been right about no cop presence ... anywhere. I had at least lucked out with my car. As I unlocked it and casually slipped inside it, he grabbed the door. My heart paused in mid-beat. "Do you have everything?" he asked as if I were returning from a sleep over.

"Yes, I seem to be altogether," I said smiling, pulling the door toward me so he would let go. When he did, I immediately locked it and started the engine. As I turned my car around, I could see in my rearview mirror Harvey was standing by "Mr. Benz," happily waving good-bye to me.

All the way back, I angrily groused aloud at myself, "How could you have let that happen? Thank your lucky stars it turned out all right in the end. You came so close to disaster. You were incredibly fortunate. Never ever leave your car again, no matter what. Cancel if you have to!" Full of remorse and suppressed fear, I put the pedal to the metal, sure I was breaking all land speed records. While I had so fervently wished to corral the local constabulary earlier, I definitely did not want to see any fuzz now. Reassuring myself, "I'm okay! I'm okay!" I made it back home safely.

At this point I had only four goals in mind. Topping the list was calling the computer dating service then attending to my hygiene. I wanted to brush my teeth and take a long hot de-contaminating shower. Then I wanted something to eat and a nap.

When I called Phase II, I asked to speak to the manager. I gave her the graphic highlights of my adventure, adding, "I strongly suggest you remove this person from your lists."

Her initial response was totally expected. It was straight out of the employees' telephone scripts manual. It was the universal strategy of countering the complaint by showing that the complainant was both cognitively wrong and a social deviant.

She said, "But *no one else* has *ever* complained about him *before*."

I wasn't going to debate this. If others had complained, they likewise would have been have discounted. I was only a hair's breadth from having my complaint dismissed. Not so fast, missy, I thought, grinding my teeth.

"Fine," I replied, barely keeping my irritation under control. Then I laid it all on the line for her, "The liability is yours. I was kidnapped, held against my will for nearly twenty-four hours, and almost raped. If he kidnaps another of your computer daters and/or assaults her, you'll have more problems than you can handle. I guarantee you I will inform the police and the victim that I warned you about him ahead of time. This is not a threat. It is a statement of fact. Can you imagine what the newspapers would make of your complicity in his actions given my early complaint and warning?"

"Oh, yes," her voice which was rising was now filled with concern and conflict. "I ... I see what you mean. Yes, well, I see what you mean. We'll certainly take him off right away." Offhandedly she added, "He's been with us six months already anyway."

Good move, I thought, as I checked the locks on all my doors, brushed my teeth until they nearly bled, and turned on the shower. I was looking forward to the lunch (dinner and breakfast) I never had and some much-needed sleep *after* I requested my phone be unlisted. From now on ... it was my way or the highway.

* *

Resulting Awareness: It had finally made a deep impression that I truly had to play it safe, not just talk about it. I had to listen to both my rational side and intuition and act on what they told me. Being even slightly unassertive because of I feared some man might negatively evaluate me was too dangerous. I was giving him power over me—my feelings, thoughts, and actions. It was making his assessment of me more important than my own. My first priority had to be to take control, to value and protect myself, irrespective of how he might feel about me as a result.

The question I asked myself: How would I now assess who was "wrong" and who was "right" to attract and date? What more meaningful criteria could I use?

* * *

New Mexico

23

DONALD

One morning I received an email from Donald, whom I had met many years before in Massachusetts. He had one of the sexiest natural speaking voices I had ever heard. It was resonant, well-modulated, and bespoke easy confidence. In spite of the fact that just hearing his voice could turn my thoughts to more profane imaginings, I was never interested in him as anything more than a friend. About six-four and two hundred pounds, with thinning and retreating brown hair, and blue eyes, he had a sweet baby face that belied his more "prurient" interests. After searching the Internet to locate me, he told me he had decided we needed to re-introduce ourselves.

Even though we had infrequently corresponded over the years, the last time I had seen him since Massachusetts was a result of his calling me at Scripps Clinic. He had been in Southern California to visit his brother in Laguna Beach. Flirtatiously, he indicated that he really wanted to see me too. However, it soon became clear what his real purpose was in our meeting again. He wanted me to take him and his brother to Disneyland ... in *my* car.

Despite my disillusionment, I thought the excursion could be fun. I hadn't been to Disneyland in nearly a year. However, if I were to be employed as their designated driver, I indicated he had to pay my admission to the park. Donald wasn't thrilled but acceded. His brother was staying with a friend on Acacia Drive which looked on the map like a piece of cake to find. Driving up Route 1 to Laguna Beach was simple. Once in the town, I turned right on Broadway, across from the main beach, and left on Acacia. However, I was unprepared for what actually lay there in front of me.

One-way Acacia had an approximately thirty-degree rise. As I looked through my windshield at it, I became anxious. I wasn't sure whether my car or I was up to it. This road made me feel as if I were going to be climbing a six-story ladder, hand-over-hand, going straight up without a safety harness. Just gazing at it, I could feel my body being pulled backwards by gravity.

At the bottom of the hill, I stopped. With no traffic I rolled back about ten feet, revved up my two-tone green 1962 Ford, and tore up the hill. Half-way up the steep grade my car stopped. The engine had stalled. I felt suspended, as if the front of the car were hanging precariously by a crane. I hunched over the steering wheel, unconsciously hoping that my action could somehow magically keep the front end of the car on the road, instead of falling over backward. Recoiling in humiliation, I thought maybe the car wasn't going to be able to make this incline. I was sure people must climb this stretch every day. Donald's brother lived up there. And they were waiting for me.

Sweating profusely as my heart pounded, I slowly backed down Acacia, my head twisted over my right shoulder, with my right calf muscle cramping as I firmly glued my foot to the brake pedal. It took me what seemed like hours to descend. Once again at the bottom, I felt so thankful to be on level ground that I could have knelt and kissed the macadam. But I still had to scale the hill. They were depending upon me. I'd have to try again ... only harder.

With one foot on the accelerator and one foot on the brake, I gunned the motor as fast as it would go. Releasing the now-smoking brakes, I raced up the hill. A cloud of burning oil was thrown up behind me. The smell coated my nasal mucosa even with the windows closed.

As I approached the crest of the hill, my car began to slow to a crawl. Inch by inch I crept closer to the top. My foot was still securely pushing the gas pedal to the floor. Another inch ... than another ... and ... I had made it! I was on firm, level ground again. I felt joyous at having met the challenge and conquered it! However, I imagined half my fuel had been incinerated during this stunt.

When I met Donald and his brother, Bob, I described my terrible driving ordeal—what I had overcome ... just for them—my red face shining, and my body damp with the sweat of victory. To my astonishment and chagrin, Bob belatedly informed me, "You should have come up Cliff Drive and cut over to Cypress or taken Aster to Cypress. Nobody comes up Acacia." What? I could have avoided that Evel Knievel ski jump altogether? And it had not occurred to anyone to make sure I knew about Acacia ahead of time? Hardly a trivial piece of information, it would have prevented the heavy wear and tear on my car's brakes and my cardiovascular system.

Donald and Bob were not the only ones present. To my surprise Bob's roommate and three other people suddenly materialized. Chatting and laughing, they unexpectedly piled into my car. No one had asked me if I minded taking a bunch of strangers as well as Donald and Bob. Apparently, I simply had been volunteered as "transportation." I introduced myself to all assembled and we left, squished together. We headed north through Newport Beach and Costa Mesa, followed Route 55 east to Interstate 5 north, and then in Anaheim turned onto Harbor Boulevard to Disneyland and a ride on Space Mountain.

Attracting and Dating the Wrong Men?

Over the years when I occasionally heard from Donald, he always "humorously" hinted at our having a more intimate relationship, starting with phone sex. Though I never took it seriously, it still made me wonder what he was really suggesting. When he next contacted me in New Mexico, he was living in West Palm Beach, Florida. A retired New York public relations executive, he was flying here for a week's conference in Albuquerque and wanted to visit with me the following weekend. I agreed to play tour guide and drive him around both Albuquerque and Santa Fe to see some of the more interesting sights—some of which I had not even visited myself yet.

First we traveled north of Santa Fe to Tesuque to visit the Shidoni Foundry. One of the country's small quality foundries, it boasted eight grassy, cottonwood-tree-lined acres adorned with a huge outdoor sculpture garden, bronze statues from the foundry, and their indoor gallery. The gallery represented more than one hundred forty artists from all over the country. The huge outdoor sculptures rising into the sky encompassed the abstract, the functional, kinetic, and realistic forms, often in dazzling colors. The breadth of imagination presented there was truly awe-inspiring.

As we walked all around the grounds, Donald directed me to take photos of particular pieces he found intriguing. He said these were for the television program he had been working on for years that he had told me about over time. Using my Nikon camera would provide better definition than his cell phone camera. Next we toured the foundry itself which poured, on average, ten thousand pounds of bronze a month. An intense heat-searing pour was taking place as we wandered through at the tail end of guided group. The actual creation of the separate pieces making up a life-size horse and rider held our attention. Artistry, chemistry, and physics combined with engineering to render something of unimaginable and gigantic beauty. Some pieces of this composition weighed several hundred pounds each.

In a workshop next to the pouring area these separate pieces were being seamlessly welded together. One finished sculpture, which stood outside the large open doors of the room as if part of the sculpture garden, was of an acrobat leaping onto the back of a galloping horse. It reminded me of a Chagall painting. Donald engaged the foundry manager, asking him questions, getting his business card, and telling him he might want to do his television program from there.

Next to the foundry, on the property to the right as you entered the Shidoni grounds, was the Tesuque Glass Works. They offered glass-blowing demonstrations each day using a variety of techniques by different artists. After we watched vases, bowls, and flowers in a startling array of colors being blown, Donald talked with the manager of its storefront, got his card, and asked about filming his show there as well.

From there we drove into Santa Fe proper to explore the shops on the Plaza on foot. It was in one high-end jewelry store that we spent the most time. As Donald talked at length with an attractive, thirtyish salesperson about his proposed show, I stood there, next to him, looking at the necklaces on display. When it was obvious I was not going to be included in their conversation, I wandered around, more carefully examining their intricately crafted earrings, rings, necklaces, bracelets, and other accessories in their many glistening glass cases.

Upon my return, Donald was speaking in greater detail about the construction of the educational television program he had designed around the sciences, arts, and adventure. She seemed intrigued by his tales of media creation. Of course, he was a potential commission on the hoof. She could afford to listen enrapt. Donald, on the other hand, was blatantly intrigued by her seeming intrigue. He was doing his utmost not to appear as though he was flirting with her as flagrantly as he was.

Approaching them from the left, I managed to subtly reform the twosome into a threesome. As if to acknowledge my presence, Donald turned to me and made a grandiose sweep of his hand over the entire seven-foot glass case in front of him. Nonchalantly he said, "What appeals to you? What would you like to have? Pick out anything you like—anything at all."

Surprised by his behavior, I did a small double-take. He was making me a collaborator in his continuing "I'm a TV producer" theatrical performance. I didn't want to take any part in it, but I wasn't sure what to do now that he had hit the ball into my court. I hated his putting me in that position. Playing along until I could comfortably disengage myself, I chose to point out a heavy, burnished silver and black onyx necklace with a hefty price tag. "This is quite attractive and so beautifully crafted," I commented and received it into my hands to examine it more closely. "And it's only two thousand dollars," I said off-handedly, for Donald's benefit, as if it would be a bargain at twice the price.

Not missing a beat, he said, "Yes, that's quite lovely. Price is no object," he added, shrugging off the hefty tab. "Is that the one you want?"

I smiled to myself but looked as if I were seriously contemplating it. Waiting barely thirty seconds, I responded, as he had expected me to. "No," I said casually, looking at other pieces, "although it's quite artistic, I'm not sure it's what I have in mind." I let him off the hook.

"If you're *really* sure?" he replied, pushing it.

"Yes," I replied smiling blandly as if this were an everyday occurrence.

Even though I really wanted to let Donald sweat for a while, as if I had mistakenly thought he truly wanted to spend two thousand dollars on me, I didn't want to contribute further to his charade. I knew that if I had actually said, "Yes, I want this," he would have had a "seizure," suffered a "myocardial infarction," or simply dropped in a "dead faint" on the highly-polished hardwood floor so he would have been unable to make the purchase. In my meaner moments I wished I had called his bluff then and there and watched him struggle awkwardly and ignominiously to get out of it.

That this was indeed a bluff was not conjecture on my part. Before he arrived in Albuquerque, Donald had said on the phone, "I've heard about that luxurious Japanese spa in the mountains in Santa Fe. I want us to go there, spend the entire day, and do all that they offer—mud baths, massages, anything and everything." He was talking about spending a carload of cash at the expensive, exclusive Japanese Spa and Resort, "Ten Thousand Waves," on Hyde Park Road in Santa Fe. I had heard of it in passing and had never thought about going, primarily because of the cost.

They offered unique treatments, such as deluxe herbal wraps, a "salt glow," which mixed mineral-rich sea salt with warm massage oil applied to your entire body, special foot and other body-parts' massages, and baths of all kinds, both communal and private which would have especially appealed to Donald. Therapeutic massages for two by themselves were over two hundred dollars.

So when he suggested he wanted to take me there, I was of two minds. While it sounded like fun, I felt uncomfortable about the financial extravagance and the serious implications for me of saying "yes." Because Donald always talked about sex and alluded to himself as a sexual adventurer, he would have expected a sexual quid pro quo for anything beyond compensating me for my time, effort, gasoline, and wear and tear on the car. But if he had wanted to do something small for me there, like a thirty-dollar foot massage, I wouldn't have argued too strenuously.

I sent him the link to their website so he could learn precisely what they offered and then make reservations for whatever he decided for himself and something inexpensive for me. A day went by as I smiled, thinking about going to "Ten Thousand Waves." It would be fun, and special. I admitted I was looking forward to it. The next day he called again, this time making a stunning announcement, "I want *you* to make all the arrangements ... and pay for them."

I couldn't quite grasp what he was communicating. Something was definitely amiss. It gave me a very queasy feeling. Donald had been given a Midas-touched, golden parachute when he retired from his famous Manhattan-headquartered PR agency. I knew he lived a very comfortable life, his wife was an executive with a chemical firm, and he was not the least bit averse to spending money on himself. I did not have two hundred dollars to spend on two massages, much less the wherewithal for a full day's worth of spa treatments.

But even if I had had the money, I was uncomfortable about his actually reimbursing me. Something I had noticed over the years was that Donald had a tendency to promise to do things and not "remember" to do them. When I questioned him about his wanting me to do it all, he said, "I don't want the expenditure to show up on my credit card bill." That told me if he wasn't willing to pay for even two massages for us, he certainly wasn't willing to pay ten times that amount for a piece of jewelry for me.

Off the Plaza, we next went to a gallery exhibiting exotic woods artistry that was of interest to both Donald and me. There he and the tall, slim, white-bearded, elderly proprietor discussed at length involving the store and its currently-featured artist in his program. The artist had on display large carved bowls of unusual shapes, often out of the Pacific Northwest's madrone burl or some hard-to-obtain wood. Some pieces were out of exotic hardwoods such as Brazilian jatoba and imbuia; Africa's West Coast bubinga; Bolivian rosewood; Mexican cocobolo; South American monterillo; and Honduran machiche. There was also Hawaiian koa which is grown in volcanic soil and known for its iridescence. Spectacularly, this wood ranges in luscious colors from tan to gold to red with brown and black accents and seems to shimmer.

The artist's abstract wood sculptures called me to examine them from every angle. Each piece was individual and extremely sensuous to the touch, whispering to me, inviting me to stroke it. Even though every piece was in excess of the price of that necklace, Donald told me in the proprietor's hearing, "Pick out something for yourself. Choose whatever you like." This time I said immediately, "There's too much from which to choose for me to make a quick decision." I had no intention to string the owner along even for a moment. This ostentatious demonstration of his so-called "largess" was getting old fast.

In talking about the artist, Donald learned he was reclusive. He disliked interviews and certainly didn't want to be filmed. At Donald's behest the proprietor was going to contact the sculptor for possible further contact by Donald. So as a favor, but mostly out of curiosity, I said I'd follow up the week after Donald had left for Florida. Speaking again with the shop owner, I secured all the pertinent information then personally contacted the sculptor, opening up the lines of communication. Beginning to sound enthusiastic, he actually agreed to be interviewed and have a film crew record how he worked. I was so pleased. It felt like a coup. Later, however, I discovered that Donald didn't follow through. I felt guilty about the part I naïvely had played in his game.

The next day we took the Sandia Peak Tramway in Albuquerque, the world's longest tramway. It had been constructed in 1966 by Bell Engineering out of Lucerne, Switzerland. Because of the steep and rocky terrain, the engineers considered it their most difficult tramway construction. It is located on Sandia Peak in the Cibola National Forest to the east of the city. Before ascending to the top, Donald talked for about twenty minutes with the engineers who ran and maintained the tram and all its electrical and mechanical components. They gave us a small tour. He then spoke with the supervisor about his filming them for his television show. The gears, wheels, and pulleys were huge and the noise even from their smooth, fluid movement was deafening. Scrutinizing the guts of this machinery, I marveled at this enormous achievement.

The actual ride to the peak was slow and scenic. Perched at the top was High Finance, the restaurant two point seven miles up and overlooking all of Albuquerque and the Rio Grande Valley. The tram ride actually took us through several climate zones as it reached its 10,378-foot elevation. From the ten-person Plexiglas-enclosed gondola I could see coyotes climbing amid the scrub, deer clambering over the rocks, as well as nature hikers and backpackers below navigating its many trails. Looking out over the city at dinner, we imbibed the last vestiges of the claret-like sunset which had set the sky afire with striations of reds and gold beneath a deepening purple coverlet.

Following the tram ride back down the mountain, I took Donald to his airport hotel room, from which he would take an early flight out in the morning to Miami International Airport. Feeling particularly randy after a day of making sexual hints, he tried to initiate a wrestling match as I was about to depart. Earlier that afternoon in Santa Fe he had already made a half-hearted attempt at sticking his hand down my bra as we stood by ourselves in the courtyard of an adobe building. I didn't find his big show of lechery all that erotic. Fortunately for me, this wrestling match likewise seemed more like some "I'm too sexy for my shirt" role he had taken on only to impress me.

After he had returned home, and to his wife, he phoned me to tell me about a fantasy he had been developing about me. The objective of the call, he said, was to determine how willing I would be to let him play it out in reality. I wondered how many others had been on the receiving end of his sharing his daytime wet dreams.

With his imagination reaching celestial heights on Viagra, he said, "With the lights low and lighted aromatic candles heightening the mood, I will tie you hand and foot spread-eagle to a bed with red silken scarves. I'll use another of these silken scarves to blindfold you. As the *Phantom of the Opera* plays loudly in the background, I'm going to slowly cut off all your clothing."

He paused as if savoring his Bettie-Page-bondage image. "I'll start by cutting holes in your top with a pair of sharp scissors to expose your breasts. I'll fondle and lick them and tickle them with my tongue and suck your nipples as you writhe in delight." Suddenly the rape scene in *A Clockwork Orange* disquietingly came to my mind.

"Next I'll cut out the crotch of your pants to lick and suck you until you can't stand it another moment and beg me to take you. Then slowly, tantalizingly, I'll cut off all your clothing, stripping your body of fabric piece by piece, stroking and caressing you until you are ready to scream with pleasure. Then I'll plunge into you over and over and over again to the swelling, passionate crescendos of the music, leaving you totally spent but pleading and crying out for more."

If he thought I'd actually let anyone tie me up, blindfold me, and allow myself to be totally under the control of someone with surging hormones who wanted to use sharp implements around my more intimate parts, he wasn't just imaginative, he was delusional. Needless to say, I didn't help him make his fantasy a reality and, apparently from what I gathered, neither did his wife. While his TV show never came to fruition, I suspected his fantasies were more than likely to have done so.

Attracting and Dating the Wrong Men?

* *

Resulting Awareness: I had known pretty much from the start that Donald was not authentic and was a user. I had gone along with him to a degree for the ride. Doing so was fun in that I had never before witnessed anyone pull what seemed to me like a con. His behavior spoke volumes about his personality. His making me a part of his game-playing, however, made me uncomfortable even if it wouldn't actually hurt anyone. Consequently, I removed myself as quickly as possible. Through my experiences with him, I found I was getting better at objectively observing men's behaviors, stepping back to rationally and intuitively ask myself how I felt about them, and what I wanted to do as a result. I was thinking more from my own personal perspective than from my father's perspective or men's gender role expectations of me. I, not he, was then the one to decide what *I* was going to do.

The question I asked myself: How was I going to continue to feel confident to direct my own actions?

* * *

24

BILL

If you've ever thought about how liberating it would be to just once break free, to do something totally spontaneous, libertine, and secretly *au natural*, you know how beguiling that feeling can be. But, sometimes, those wonderfully-pleasurable, hedonic expectations and cold reality collide head-on, leaving you slaked but emotionally un-liberated.

It started with my unmitigated delight that the all-too-infrequent cumulonimbus clouds were finally forming themselves overhead in our July–to–September monsoon season. This meant central New Mexico had a better than even chance at receiving some desperately needed precipitation. Until this occurred, vegetation and wild animals were frequently suffering and some dying as a result of the intense heat, dryness, and high level of ultraviolet radiation. But now the clouds were rapidly building slate-bottomed cities of towering skyscrapers.

They hung heavily above the fiery air and parched land, portending sweet, glorious rain. Then the sky erupted. Explosively thunderous clashes cannonaded. Electrical discharges fingered the darkening apricot and lavender sky. Like neural dendrites they reached out for cell bodies in other clouds and in the earth. The air crackled with foreboding. The heavens were putting on their showiest spectacle. On tenterhooks, the earth, plants, and animals awaited the inexorable, arroyo-creating deluge. In an instant rain slammed and pockmarked the earth

Attracting and Dating the Wrong Men?

I had spent the day sticking to my home office chair with sweat un-esthetically running down between my breasts. I was putting together a seminar on effective ways to confidently overcome fear of self-presentation. As the large, heavy droplets violently lashed the floor-to-ceiling windows which overlooked my back deck, I was deliriously drawn to its promised release. Imagining its seductively cool invitation, I threw off my clothes. Hurriedly I left them in a heap on the living room brick floor and I opened the glass back door.

High winds swirled and pelted the rain against my skin, magnetically drawing me outward. The feeling was indescribably erotic. Without a second thought, I raced onto the wall-protected deck to luxuriate in Nature's wildness. Thirty-five-mile an hour gusts made the rain even more lusciously and savagely invigorating. I felt a part of Nature. I was Nature's child, my own inner child. I was no longer the being I was expected and required to be every day. I was at one with the universe.

As I frenziedly danced around on the redwood decking, I let the droplets slap and tickle every inch of skin. Total freedom, it was better than sex. As a whirlwind twisted my hair around, whipping my face and shoulders, it also caught the glass door. It slammed shut with a resounding thud. I was too intoxicated and giddy to notice. As the storm raged on, the air was now becoming chilled. My body temperature was dropping too. Every millimeter of my skin's erectile tissue was standing at attention. My drenched hair which was streaming down my face and back was adding to it. With my body spent and rapidly cooling, I began to shiver. I needed to head back inside. But to my mortification, I couldn't. In my haste to get outside, I hadn't checked the door lock. The lock had set.

I knew this wasn't a big problem—a little embarrassing, perhaps—because Bill, my long-time companion whom I had known from Massachusetts, was in his office just off the living room. He was busy assassinating aliens on his computer, playing *Doom*. I knocked. No response. I knocked again, harder. There was still no response. I slammed my fist onto the wooden door frame with such force that the single glass pane seemed to tremble in its housing. I called, "Hey, let me in!" I could hear the sounds of Bill's cyber-gun as he demolished slavering monsters, reducing them to puddles of gore. I started pounding on the door repeatedly. With the game's blasting sound effects he couldn't hear another thing.

My shaking body was now breaking out in large goose bumps. It was obvious that the only way inside was for me to circle around to the front. That meant traversing the snake- and rat-infested jungle walk on the west side of the house, slipping through the coyote-fence-enclosed garden, crossing the broad gravel driveway into the front courtyard, and ringing the ear-piercing front doorbell which I knew would get his attention.

In the low light from the living room overhead bulbs automatically dimmed I edged my way down the deck steps by feel. At the hand-carved wooden gate in the back stucco-walled courtyard, I released it, edged through, and reset it to help keep out the coyotes and neighborhood dogs. I turned left on the rocky soil toward the foot-worn path beside the house. Because of the steep incline on the east side of the house, there was no path there. Sharp stones, dead, dry plant stalks, and sand burs stabbed my bare feet. Long, slender drooping branches of the New Mexico willow on the right outer edge of the path lasciviously brushed my now-violently quaking body.

As I tried quickening my step, I stumbled over river rock which had been placed under the canales, box-shaped wooden and metal spouts from the roof. They directed drainage from the slightly-canted, "flat" Pueblo-style roof toward the deep arroyo to my right. The water pouring heavily from above further soaked and refrigerated my body. Even though the moon and stars were beginning to appear in the sky, the heavy cloud cover obscured their light. Only window-blind-muted illumination from my office helped me avoid a large river rock that had been dislodged. If I had tripped over it, I would likely have been pitched head-first down the arroyo's embankment into the fast-moving water below which was further excavating its sandy channel. Once past that, I was plunged into darkness again.

Something leapt out at me, piercing my ankle. "Oh, my God! A snake?" My heart skipped a couple of beats. Rattlers abounded in this desert area. I had seen many of them under the junipers that lined our gravel driveway and looking for mice in the garden. While I didn't expect one to be out in the rain at night, I had to know if I had been struck. If so, I'd have to tie off my lower leg with whatever I could find until I could get to the ER as soon as possible. Cautiously I lowered my hand to my ankle. My fingers touched metal. I sighed with deeply-felt relief. The culprit was a folded, discarded chicken-wire plant cage that had previously encircled a large desert marigold. As I trod on it, it had twisted up and stabbed me. As I continued slowly step by step, holding my breath, I kept my left arm extended with my hand reaching for the exterior stucco wall of the house. As long as I could touch it, I had two feet to spare from the arroyo edge.

When I arrived at the back garden gate, I exhaled. Once inside the garden, I was on the sandstone walk which allowed me to move along more quickly. All I had to do was follow its smooth surface as it wound around plantings until I approached the large rustic barn-board gate leading to the driveway. But there I was abruptly stopped. The area was bathed in bright light. Headlights were flashing. Neighbors were retrieving their mail from the community boxes at the head of our long, inclined drive.

Rubbing my upper arms to warm myself, I waited expectantly as three cars in succession klieg-lighted my path. "Come on, come on," I muttered between my now-chattering teeth. I needed to make a frantic dash to the high-walled front courtyard before another car appeared. One, two, and then the third car left. With the three cars now on their way and no sign of lights from the main road coming into the top of the loop on which our house was situated, I slowly opened the heavy door. Slipping through, I tried to do the impossible—run.

I hadn't taken the gravel size into my calculations. Oohing, owing, and squeaking in pain, I delicately pranced over the sharp medium-sized pieces, raising my legs high. My body inelegantly bounced and jounced along with my trotting cadence. Then a car suddenly roared down the main road. It turned a sharp right. Headlights illuminated our driveway. My rain-sequined body shimmered in the light. There was no cover. I was half-way, caught, exposed, stuck. But worrying about someone happening to view my "nude, avant-garde dance performance" was the last thing on my mind. I was concerned about hypothermia.

At the front courtyard, I threw open the sandblasted gate and ran on tiptoes on the flagstone walkway to the sconce-lighted stoop. I was finally out of the rain. There I jammed my thumb into the doorbell button ... and held it there.

Freezing minutes passed slowly. I hopped up and down from one foot to the other. I wrapped my arms tightly around my upper torso, my hands again trying to circulate some warm blood back into my upper arms. I waited for Bill to arrive. The six-panel cedar door opened a few inches. Bill peered out as if to see who could be visiting at that hour, unannounced, in the storm. When he saw me, he stared. It was as if he were mesmerized by the sight of this comically soggy, goose-bumpy apparition. Seconds passed. Not waiting, I rushed past him, waving my hand to spurn any possible questions.

Now wrapped in a blanket, I had an aha! The key to success is going after what you want according to your own values and expectations ... but having a lock pick handy wouldn't hurt!"

* *

Resulting Awareness: My not caring what Bill thought about my current physical state and the behavior that led up to it told me I was deciding for myself what my goals were and how I would achieve them. It told me that I wasn't acting according to his expectations but to my own. I didn't need his permission and I didn't need to make excuses for what I had done. That likewise applied to my complying with my father's embedded dictates and his gender-role expectations of me. From here on out I could use my own assessments of situations in order to decide what to do. Even feeling like a cold, drowned rat, I was, in truth one happy camper!

* * *

EPILOGUE

As those of you who have already made this journey—or are currently in the throes of it—already know, it's a tough slog to get from unaware to aware, dependent to independent, unassertive to assertive, from forbiddance to permission, from meeting others' expectations to meeting your own. Through my fifteen years of attracting and dating the wrong men, I learned what I didn't know but needed to and what I had to do to finally deal with men comfortably and satisfactorily.

I came to recognize that gender role expectations existed in the culture and in my unconscious. I saw not only that they interfered with my asserting my autonomy but also that I could ultimately step outside my loyalty, acceptance of and adherence to them. It required my looking at and analyzing each belief that was standing in my way. I discovered I didn't have to play that game any longer.

The hard lesson I learned was that I could choose to ignore what my culture, parents, teachers, church, television, and advertising had drummed into my head about how I was "supposed to meet men's expectations." Irrespective of my unconscious loyalties to those gender-role and family expectations, I had individual, non-gender-related rights that I could express, especially in my female-male relationships. I could give myself permission to be disloyal to those beliefs that were keeping me from being the *real* me. It became a matter of recognizing, accepting, and then acting on these rights.

I discovered I had the right to ask for what I wanted, to say "no" to things I did not want, and not to have to put up with people who tried to manipulate and control me because they felt they could place their needs and wants above mine. I discovered I had the right to have and express my own opinions and not defer to people simply because they happened to have the external plumbing I didn't. In sum, I discovered I had the right to respect and accept myself unconditionally as I was—with all my faults, strengths, and virtues. I also had the right to be treated with respect and as an equal to men in these attraction and dating situations. In essence, I could then choose to be any version of Wonder Woman I wanted, with or without the Golden Lasso of Truth, the white-striped red boots, and bullet-deflecting cuffs.

It was only when I could see why I was doing what I was doing in my interactions with men, I could stop trying to mold myself to how men expected me to act toward them. I could accomplish what *I* wanted ... the way I wanted to. I could finally define myself by my own standards. I could comfortably present and "advertise" myself as the real me with confidence and pride—*what you see is what you get*—and then, like Harriet, let men decide if that were of interest to them.

And once I recognized all this, *I acted on this awareness ... little by little.* I chose my own path, free of past allegiances and forbiddances. I acted to free, embolden, and empower myself to do whatever I felt was necessary to make things work for *me* within *my* beliefs. Doing so finally allowed me to enjoy attracting and dating men. Now I could consciously, joyously dance with abandon in the rain rather than unconsciously miserably just get soaked.

No matter where you are in the attracting-dating process, you too can discover how to get rid of your unconscious hold-backs and give yourself permission to avoid attracting and dating the wrong men. You too can free, embolden, and empower yourself to attract and date the *right* men!

ABOUT THE AUTHOR

Signe A. Dayhoff, PhD, MA, MEd, is a social psychologist from Boston University with post-graduate training in counseling, emotional intelligence, and positive psychology. For over 30 years she has been a cognitive-behaviorist, coach, educator, and author, specializing in increasing interpersonal communication and self-confidence, alleviating social anxiety, and improving relationships.

She has taught psychology at Boston University, University of Massachusetts, and Framingham State College and has done research at Massachusetts Institute of Technology, Scripps Clinic and Research Foundation, and Fairview State Hospital, presenting nationally her research on social anxiety, social effectiveness, and mentoring/networking.

She is author of seventeen books, including *What Faust the Dancing Cat Taught Me; Growing Up "Unacceptable"—How Katharine Hepburn Rescued Me; How Insiders Get Jobs: 6-Mini-Course Series; Scared of Your Boss? Smash Through Your Fear Now; Promote Myself? I'd Rather Eat Worms!; How to Speak Without Fear Small Talk Course*; the new and improved 2nd Ed. of *Diagonally-Parked in a Parallel Universe: Working Through Social Anxiety* (2010), (the social phobic's bible and insider's scoop, which has been praised by noted clinical researchers); *Create Your Own Career Opportunities; Get The Job You Want;* and *Decision Making For Managers.* And she contributed to David Riklan's *101 Great Ways to Improve Your Life (Vol. 2)* and Steven J. Bennett's *Executive Chess: Creative Problem Solving By 45 of America's Top Business Leaders and Thinkers.*

Attracting and Dating the Wrong Men?

An applied feline behaviorist and rescuer, she is kitty-mom to 20-plus senior cats, consults, writes, and speaks on improving human-cat relationships from both the human and cat's communication perspective and the human-animal bond.

www.ingramcontent.com/pod-product-compliance
Lightning Source LLC
Chambersburg PA
CBHW060822050426
42453CB00008B/545